HANDS ON, MINDS ON

How Executive Function, Motor, and Spatial Skills Foster School Readiness

CLAIRE E. CAMERON

Foreword by Sharon Ritchie

TEACHERS COLLEGE PRESS

TEACHERS COLLEGE | COLUMBIA UNIVERSITY

NEW YORK AND LONDON

Published by Teachers College Press, 1234 Amsterdam Avenue, New York, NY 10027

Copyright © 2018 by Teachers College, Columbia University Claire E. Cameron

Cover design by adam b. bohannon. Cover photos by vwpix / Adobe Stock.

Library of Congress Cataloging-in-Publication Data is available at loc.gov

ISBN 978-0-8077-5909-7 (paper)
ISBN 978-0-8077-7694-0 (ebook)

Printed on acid-free paper
Manufactured in the United States of America

25   24   23   22   21   20   19   18   8   7   6   5   4   3   2   1

HANDS ON,
MINDS ON

For Chris and Simon

Contents

PART III: LINKING THE LEARNING DOMAINS AND THE FOUNDATIONAL COGNITIVE SKILLS

Foreword

As an educator who very much appreciates the contributions of brain research to the conversation about what should happen for young children in school settings, I was delighted to have the opportunity to read this book. Teachers, both novice and veteran, are eager to learn how to apply brain research to their practice, and Dr. Cameron has offered some very real knowledge and support to this effort. Although teachers seem to have infinite patience for teaching children skills such as counting and letter and word identification, too often, when the foundational cognitive skills that Dr. Cameron addresses here are missing or underdeveloped, children are disciplined rather than supported. This book provides the kind of thinking needed for a broader definition of what it really means to teach young learners and helps educators recognize the need to make certain these areas are explicitly and regularly addressed as opportunities for learning and development.

Dr. Cameron begins by addressing the issue of school readiness through the lens of cognitive skills, moves into a thorough examination and description, and finishes by linking these skills to learning domains. Her main goals are to demonstrate how three foundational cognitive skills (executive function, motor skills, and spatial skills) support children's learning and to advocate for full and rich early academic and nonacademic experiences that incorporate them in daily practice. Her thorough review of the research that underlies her thinking is both helpful and instructive. Educators must have the tools and ability to advocate for their students, who are often mired in systems that have neither the knowledge base nor the time or interest to provide the policy and financial support needed to make sure young children are provided high-quality experiences. This reality, as we all know, is even more common for children of color and those who come from less-advantaged homes. Arming educators with research and the ability to articulate the research on behalf of their students is crucial to ongoing efforts to achieve equity.

The descriptions of a variety of assessments that help identify children's needs in executive function, motor skills, and spatial skills are invaluable. Dr. Cameron presents tables that allow readers to view the ideas presented in synthesized and engaging ways. In addition, she provides vignettes at the beginning of the chapters to give readers a lens through which to organize their thinking, and then concludes with a summary where the children's needs are addressed in concrete ways. Readers are urged to consider these skills both as something children possess and as something whose development is supported or constrained by children's learning environments and interactions both at school and at home. This organized yet varied approach allows for a very fast-paced read and gives each reader a chance to think about the content in a variety of formats.

I am personally very pleased to have this book in my possession. Dr. Cameron reframes and details ideas in ways that provide me with the thinking and examples I need to enhance practice for the hundreds of teachers I encounter on a regular basis. I can now move from what I have viewed as rather rudimentary and simplistic approaches to a far more sophisticated, relevant, and helpful approach. I thank Dr. Cameron for providing me with this resource, and I believe that you will thank her as well.

—Sharon Ritchie

Preface

In this book, I examine school readiness in the United States by synthesizing scientific research on *executive function, motor skills*, and *spatial skills*. A growing body of research establishes that these three skill sets form the basis for young children to make a strong academic, behavioral, and social transition to a formal learning environment. I endeavor to show how these skill sets—which I usually call "skills" for simplicity—are *foundational* to learning in early childhood and explain the research on their *cognitive* underpinnings.

Most children in the United States make the transition to kindergarten when they are 5 years old, but the transition to formal schooling also encompasses the years before and after kindergarten entry. Therefore, I describe research from preschool (ages 3 to 5 years), kindergarten (age 5), and 1st through 3rd grade (ages 6 to 8). Most experts call the span from 3 to 8 years the early childhood period. In a very few cases where research on this period is limited, I describe studies conducted with 9- and 10-year-olds.

Keeping in mind what makes a healthy and productive classroom learning environment for young children, in my research I have mainly focused on what I call *child factors*, especially those skills that are possible to measure by asking children to perform certain tasks, answer certain questions, or demonstrate certain competencies.

Child factors make a huge difference in the success that children have when they enter school. Behavioral, cognitive, and social skills affect how children function in the classroom and relate with their peers and teachers. What's more, whether children can perform tasks with ease or frustration—and whether their efforts lead to learning and success or to more frustration—informs how they see themselves, how they see school, and how schools and teachers see them.

Because executive function, motor skills, and spatial skills are not well known among early childhood professionals and policymakers, my first goal in writing this book is to introduce these skills to non-research, educational audiences. My primary audience is pre- and inservice teachers and teacher educators. I provide concrete examples and a review of the available scientific evidence in cognitive, developmental, and educational psychology, among other fields, including economics, physical and occupational thera-py, clinical psychology, and special education.

Even though this book focuses on child factors, I also show how young children's skills, abilities, knowledge, emotions, and behaviors are inherent-ly *context dependent* and *dynamic*.

Context dependent means that what children can do in the classroom is shaped by their families, community, and related experiences up until the point of assessment. *Dynamic* means that young children's skills are almost always changing—sometimes improving, sometimes appearing to decline—and so are difficult to predict. In other words—as any teacher knows—children often surprise us.

At the same time, hundreds of research studies from education, psychol-ogy, sociology, and other fields have established that by the time children enter kindergarten, those from middle- and upper-socioeconomic status (SES) backgrounds far outpace those from low-SES backgrounds in school readiness. Skill disparities are evident across assessments of familiar aca-demic skills and behavioral readiness for the classroom, as well as the three foundational cognitive skills that are the focus of this book.

SES-related differences in children's performance are most commonly known as achievement gaps. Unfortunately, the term *achievement gap* hides what is really going on. Most experts agree that differences in academic achievement between the nation's most and least advantaged children arise not from within children themselves but from unequal early learning en-vironments and experiences. So, achievement gaps—and their disquieting cousins, behavioral gaps and the discipline gap—arise from what are more accurately called *learning opportunity gaps*, which are driven in turn by resource and income gaps.

The wealth gap in the United States is the widest it has ever been since measurements began, with low-SES families enduring pervasive and ex-treme stress in financial, relationship, community, and health domains. Understanding how to support the most vulnerable of our young children—of whom one in five live in poverty—is imperative.

With that goal in mind, I hope this book finds its way to those profes-sionals who work with young children through schools of education and psychology classes, in courses on child development, cognitive processes involved in learning, early childhood education curricula and policy, or achievement gaps.

My aim is not to explore topics exhaustively but to synthesize the re-search that I have found most useful in my own thinking and scholarship. I hope to raise new questions and connections for readers about how to foster school readiness, especially among children from impoverished backgrounds.

A secondary goal is to familiarize readers with how researchers of early childhood development approach their profession. In other words, I would like readers to come away with a richer understanding of how research that involves young children, their teachers, and their classrooms is designed and conducted; how surveys, assessments, and observations are developed; and the type and strength of conclusions it is appropriate to draw from different types of studies.

To engage readers in thinking about how research in early childhood connects with real life, every chapter includes vignettes of early childhood classrooms, short optional exercises with active learning questions, and in-depth explanations of research studies.

This book's chapters are grouped into four parts. In Part I, I describe three views on school readiness as child-focused, context-focused, or child-and-context-focused (Chapter 1). I then review disparities in early learning environments arising from background factors such as SES and draw attention to aspects of the classroom context that contribute to whether children thrive or struggle in that setting (Chapter 2).

Along with differences in early resources and experiences, including interactions with caregivers, peers, and objects, children's readiness to learn when they begin preschool contributes to how they fare at the end of kindergarten (McWayne, Cheung, Wright, & Hahs-Vaughn, 2012). So, positive early learning experiences are especially important for those children new to school who may, when first meeting their teachers, seem the most difficult to engage productively in classroom life.

Giving children the chance to learn and practice their foundational executive function (EF), motor, and spatial skills is paramount to their succeeding in the classroom, as I take up in Part II. After all, children can't learn without being able to control their impulses, remember information, and focus and shift their attention (EF, Chapter 3); move their bodies and hands appropriately (motor skills, Chapter 4); and integrate visual and spatial information to use classroom materials and problem-solve (spatial skills, Chapter 5). These chapters introduce a multitude of technical terms. I have organized the terms associated with EF, motor skills, and spatial skills in Figure P.1, shown at the end of the Preface.

After defining each of the foundational cognitive skills, I move on in Part III to explain how EF, motor skills, and spatial skills lay foundations for learning and support children's school readiness in nonacademic areas (Chapter 6), as well as in literacy (Chapter 7) and mathematics (Chapter 8). The book's main title, *Hands On, Minds On*, refers to the many connections between foundational cognitive skills and learning in both nonacademic areas and academics in early childhood, when hands-on activities are especially appropriate. For the use of this apt phrase, I thank the Brookings Institute. Scholars there are communicating at a global level how children learn through actively engaging their bodies and minds (Roth, Kim, & Care, 2017; Winthrop, Williams, & McGivney, 2016).

Finally, in Part IV, I propose guided object play as a way to foster foundational cognitive skills, and I share findings from an after-school curriculum that used guided object play to successfully improve children's EF and spatial skills (Chapter 9). Chapter 10 concludes the book by pointing out that children with initially low skill levels benefit from learning opportunities that explicitly focus on those skills, and guided object play provides this type of explicit learning opportunity.

There are some topics that I virtually ignore. For example, I devote little space to gender and racial/ethnic differences in children's foundational cognitive skills and school readiness. The research in this area is vast, and I would not be able to do it justice with a quick gloss. More important, I believe that emphasizing demographic variables that place children into groups based on those variables is not very informative for understanding and supporting individual children.

In other words, for an early childhood professional, knowing a child's gender and race/ethnicity provides relatively little insight, compared to understanding how a child's parents interact with them; how deep, knowledgeable, and available the family's wider social network is; or whether the child has access to healthy food and stimulating, engaging, and safe pastimes.

With this claim, I don't mean to minimize the importance of race, culture, and ethnicity to one's experience of living in the United States or any other society. Research on culturally responsive pedagogy shows that it is imperative for teachers to understand the history, values, and beliefs of families and children (Reid & Kagan, 2014). From my view of the research, gender and race/ethnicity are poor substitutes for a host of more interesting environmental dynamics and differences, however. I urge teachers to learn about children's out-of-school environments by forming meaningful relationships with children's families and understanding the home cultural practices of the children in their charge.

Unfortunately, human beings do treat children differently based on their physical characteristics. Teachers may even provide different environments based on their concepts about how people with those characteristics are, should be, or can be. When our son was born, one of his relatives, who already had a granddaughter, said, "Boys are different, aren't they?" I thought, but didn't have the wherewithal to say, "*Children* are different. My child's individual qualities mean so much more than his sex parts."

While I'm on this topic: Our society's growing awareness of the fact that for some children, their sex parts don't match who they feel they are, is the reason that—whenever possible—I use *they/them/their* pronouns, instead of the binary *his/her* distinction.

Throughout this book, I emphasize how the environment can shape, constrain, or foster children's adaptive development. My main thesis proposes that early childhood professionals attend to the three foundational cognitive skills through a specific type of play: guided object play. I argue that by interweaving guided object play into children's daily routines, early childhood settings can help explicitly address the learning opportunity gaps among advantaged and disadvantaged preschoolers that result in wide achievement and behavioral gaps before kindergarten even begins.

Note that I don't advance guided object play as a panacea for all problems of school readiness. Such a mindset, which assumes there is a single skill or activity that will "fix everything," is not appropriate given the complexity of children's development across multiple intersecting skill domains during early childhood.

Instead, I present guided object play as a unifying theme to help connect, on the one hand, research results from many studies in disparate areas of children's learning and development with, on the other, the day-to-day activities of the early childhood classroom. I suggest that early childhood teachers offer children more guided object play while also calling for other necessary shifts to support children's school readiness, such as changing how we think about and invest in early childhood education as a profession.

I want to express gratitude to several people who have shaped my own learning and development: My mentors across the years (John Hagen, Fred Morrison, Carol McDonald Connor, Sara Rimm-Kaufman, and David Grissmer) and my closest collaborator in the executive function world, Megan McClelland, all deserve special thanks. And teachers know that students help us learn the most, so I thank Claire Baker, Tony Byers, and Helyn Kim for their trust in me as a research mentor, as well as my co-authors—many of whom are my closest friends—on academic publications.

For their aid specific to this book, I thank my two writing groups, both in Buffalo and Charlottesville (especially Anne Carley, Bethany Carlson, Carolyn O'Neal, Noelle Beverly, and Andrea Rowland), who uncomplainingly read and universally improved my very rough chapter drafts. My graduate student and future colleague, Amy Mace, worked all summer to scour diverse literatures and respond to my requests. I also thank Teachers College Press (Sarah Biondello and Susan Liddicoat, in particular). And I'm grateful to my parents, especially my mother, Mary Cameron Mitchell, for steady encouragement and support that included last-minute editing.

Thank you most of all to my dear spouse, Chris Rates, for making it possible for me to write a book during my first year of motherhood. Now that we are parents, this project is personal. It represents my small effort to support the dedication, resourcefulness, and love with which families and early childhood professionals care for their own young children.

Figure P.1. Three Foundational Cognitive Skills and Associated Terms

Executive Function

Inhibitory control (self-control)
Working memory
Cognitive flexibility (attentional shifting or switching)
Effortful control
Executive attention

Motor Skills

Fine motor skills
Gross motor skills
Strength and precision
Body awareness (proprioception)
Crossing the midline (bilateral integration)
Motor planning, speed, and sequencing

Spatial Skills

Perceptual skills
Spatial working memory
Transformational skills
Constructional skills
Visuo-motor integration

Part I

THINKING ABOUT SCHOOL READINESS

CHAPTER 1

Foundational Cognitive Skills and School Readiness

It's the first day in your new 4-year-old preschool classroom and you're almost ready to begin your very first circle time. You briefly notice Nadia, who sits with her hands folded on her mat, waiting for the morning activities to begin, before your attention shifts to Jean. Her mother brought Jean to school in a whirlwind of whining and fidgeting. Jean is on all fours, about to crawl from one side of the circle of mats to the other. Your teacher assistant grabs onto Jean's feet.

Then you notice Michael and Charlie, twin boys who sit side by side, their heads close together, talking intently but quietly; they hardly seem to realize they are in a classroom. Another child, Miriam, remains seated but points excitedly at the calendar, saying over and over in a loud voice, "Sunday Monday Tuesday Wednesday!"

You can't help wondering whether all these children will pass their school-readiness assessment for kindergarten. Then you remind yourself that it's your job to help them be able to do that, less than a year from now. The task feels daunting.

Starting school is both exciting and challenging for young children. The transition to formal school occurs for most children in the United States when they go to kindergarten, sometime around their 5th birthday.

For a child who is only 5 or 6 years old, adjusting to an early-morning routine, boarding a bus or riding in a car, and spending most of the day without family—while being expected to learn new and difficult skills—can be overwhelming. Even in 1st grade, some children continue to struggle with classroom expectations and to understand how to "do school."

In this book, I explore how early childhood professionals can help young children begin preschool, kindergarten, and early elementary school, and enjoy learning with their peers, teachers, and materials. This book delves into three skills that teachers at all these levels can foster by deepening their background knowledge in the skills and how they develop.

Executive function (EF), spatial skills, and especially motor skills are often mentioned in child development courses. Yet, early childhood teachers are unlikely to take professional teaching courses where they learn to *identify* and *assess* these three foundational cognitive skills or to *foster* them with certain interactions and classroom activities. After reading this book, I hope that readers are better able to identify, assess, and foster children's development in three cognitive skills that I argue are foundational for children's learning and readiness for school.

Part of serving as a "foundation" means that the cognitive processes involved in EF, motor skills, and spatial skills tend to be hidden, unless teachers know what they are looking for. After defining the foundational cognitive skills in Chapters 3 through 5, I share research showing how these skills form the basis for children to develop many other aspects of school readiness.

These other aspects include nonacademic areas such as social-emotional development, and academic areas, including literacy and mathematics learning. Virtually all the different learning areas of the early childhood developmental period connect, in some way, to at least one of the foundational cognitive skills. And whenever children get "hands on" to learn with manipulatives and other materials, they rely on their foundational cognitive skills.

Before proceeding, I first ask: *What is school readiness?* Is it something that children have, lack, or can develop? Research supports the third option: School readiness can be developed. And if school readiness can be developed, then we should focus our energies on aspects of readiness that underlie and connect to multiple areas of children's development—hence my focus on the foundational cognitive skills.

> **THEME:** School readiness emerges as children interact with a learning
> context. Further, supporting three foundational cognitive skills (EF,
> motor skills, and spatial skills) among young children can benefit
> their readiness to learn in nonacademic and academic areas.

THREE VIEWS ON SCHOOL READINESS

Defining school readiness is not an easy task, and several views of the concept exist. For example, the Head Start Early Childhood Learning and Knowledge Center's website mentions families and schools, but ultimately states that school readiness is *"children possessing* the skills, knowledge, and attitudes necessary for success in school and for later learning and life" (eclkc.ohs. acf.hhs.gov/hslc/hs/sr; emphasis added). In contrast, UNICEF defines school readiness as "three interlinked dimensions: a) ready children; b) ready schools; and c) ready families" (Rebello Britto & Limlingan, 2012, p. 3).

These two definitions are useful because they show the breadth of people and contexts invoked by the concept of school readiness. Whereas Head

Start's definition emphasizes the child, UNICEF's definition acknowledges two other "dimensions" involved: family and schools.

In this section, I review Scott-Little et al.'s (2006) three views of school readiness: a view focused primarily on the child (child-focused view); a view focused primarily on the context (context-focused view); or a view that sees the child in context (child-in-context view).

With a child-focused view, children's behaviors may appear as immutable parts of "who they are." With a context-focused view, behaviors are changeable as the situation changes. Finally, with the child-in-context view, behaviors emerge from the child's personal qualities interacting with the unique features of the situation. This third view aligns best with research on child development.

WHERE DO THE FOUNDATIONAL COGNITIVE SKILLS FIT INTO HEAD START'S SCHOOL READINESS DEFINITION?

Over 20 years ago, the National Education Goals Panel (1995) brought together experts from universities, think tanks, and advocacy organizations. This group agreed on five broad school-readiness domains, which were then adopted by the Department of Health and Human Services in 2000, and updated in 2003 (Administration on Children, Youth and Families/ Head Start Bureau, 2003). Head Start revised the framework and made it more specific (Administration on Children Youth and Families/Head Start Bureau, 2010), and then revised it a third time, to incorporate research from birth through preschool age (Administration on Children, Youth and Families/Head Start Bureau, 2015).

Despite all the revisions, today's five overarching NEGP domains are very similar to those coined in 1995, albeit with two minor wording changes: Now *Physical and Motor Development* is called *Perceptual, Motor, and Physical Development*, and *Cognition and General Knowledge* is called *Cognition*. The remaining three domains are the same: *Social and Emotional Development, Approaches Toward Learning*, and *Language and Literacy*.

In today's Head Start framework, the foundational cognitive skill of executive function appears under Approaches Toward Learning as *cognitive self-regulation*; motor skills appear in Perceptual, Motor, and Physical Development; and spatial skills are part of Cognition. But this simple sorting task belies how fundamental EF, motor skills, and spatial skills are for all of the school-readiness domains.

The idea that the three foundational cognitive skills deserve to be highlighted more in conversations about school readiness forms the basis for this book.

The Child-Focused View

Looking back at the chapter-opening vignette, based on the minimal information provided, a "child-focused question" asks which child or children in the vignette seem(s) most ready for school—quiet Nadia, fidgety Jean, enthusiastic Miriam, or the twins Michael and Charlie?

It's clear that the twins, Michael and Charlie are very close, and their tendency to avoid other children may seem to be offset by their strong relationship with each other. A teacher taking the child-focused view might decide that Michael and Charlie are shy, and that they mainly need each other to be comfortable. Similarly, Nadia seems the "most ready" because she is waiting patiently. School requires that children learn to wait, and a teacher whose definition of school readiness focuses on the child may decide that Nadia is going to have a better year than the other children.

On the one hand, it's natural for humans to make quick judgments based on initial impressions and to categorize people into groups; these quick judgments can help a teacher of 18 to 20 children learn everyone's names quickly and decide which children need the support of an adult.

But on the other, an overemphasis on child-focused views of school readiness may cause teachers to overlook new information that contradicts their initial impressions. Another problem arises when teachers' initial impressions of children override their understanding of how the context also matters for children's behavior. Thus, relying only on what children bring to the classroom masks how that context contributes to their skills and behaviors.

The Context-Focused View

The second view of school readiness is addressing whether the school or classroom is ready for the children. A "context-focused question" asks: Does the classroom context allow children to demonstrate their skills, or does it prevent them from doing so? UNICEF defines ready schools as those with "practices [that] a) foster and support a smooth transition for children to primary school and beyond; and b) promote learning for all children" (Rebello Britto & Limlingan, 2012, p. 4).

In the vignette, Miriam notices the calendar and uses it to demonstrate her knowledge of the days of the week. This choice of what material to display (a calendar) shapes the teacher's impression of Miriam's school readiness. What can't be known is, what if a poster next to the calendar showed the 20 most common signs in American Sign Language? This change in the context might have enabled Jean, whose father is deaf, to show her special expertise.

A limitation with the context-focused view is that teachers can't anticipate every possible environmental variation that would allow every child to show what they know. And children undoubtedly enter school with wide differences in temperament, language, and previous learning experiences, which influences how they interact with the people and materials in the classroom. Individual differences among children, and how these differences manifest in a variety of behaviors given a specific classroom context, are why the third view on school readiness is most aligned with the evidence I share in this book.

The Child-in-Context View

Instead of emphasizing *either* the child (child-focused view) *or* the context (context-focused view), the third conceptualization of school readiness (child-in-context view) acknowledges *both*. In other words, school readiness is what the child brings to school *and* the environmental supports, opportunities, and limitations that contribute to how the child does after school entry (Scott-Little, Kagan, & Frelow, 2006; Wesley & Buysse, 2003). Experts in child development endorse this definition as well (Bronfenbrenner & Morris, 2006; Pianta, Cox, & Snow, 2007).

As a teacher, taking the child-in-context view allows you to imagine and carry out changes to that context to try to increase the likelihood of new and more adaptive behaviors from that child.

With such a view, the following might occur: You recognize that Michael and Charlie could miss opportunities to interact with their peers if they spend most of their time with each other, and so you split them up during at least one classroom activity. And, after asking children to bring in a family tree with photos, you learn that Jean's father is deaf and the family is new to the area. Knowing this, you put the family in touch with a nonprofit that places individuals who are deaf in jobs at local businesses.

Because Jean's father goes from unemployed to employed while Jean is in your classroom, you observe that Jean—and her mother likewise—seems less frazzled and more calm and predictable in the classroom.

THREE FOUNDATIONAL COGNITIVE SKILLS AND SCHOOL READINESS

The goal of Table 1.1 is to demonstrate some practices and features of family and classroom contexts that are "hidden" behind school-readiness items posed to individual children. In column 1 are examples of six possible school-readiness items. In columns 2 and 3 are family and classroom context variables that may affect the child's performance on the item.

For example, referring to the first question, if children have alphabet magnets or lots of books at home, that will affect how many letters they can recognize in a school-readiness assessment (Morrison, Bachman, & Connor, 2005). Item 2, about counting to 20, is a common way to assess children's early number skills.

Items 3 through 6 pertain to the foundational cognitive skills that are the focus of this book: Item 3 corresponds to executive function, Items 4 and 5 to motor skills, and Item 6 to spatial skills. Each is briefly defined in the next sections and explored in more depth in Chapters 3–5.

> **EXERCISE:** Now pretend it's the middle of summer and you are an early childhood teacher administering school-readiness assessments to your future students. At the assessment, you also had the opportunity to talk with their families. Review Table 1.1 with a given child or family in mind.

Table 1.1. How Context Matters for Common School-Readiness Assessment Items

Child	Family Context	Classroom Context
1. How many letters does the child recognize?	How many books are at home?	Where in the classroom is the alphabet displayed?
2. Can the child count to 20?	Are there board games at home for the child to play with?	How often do children use numbers during the day, to count while waiting, sort materials, or estimate time?
3. Can the child sit still until the bell rings?	At mealtimes, does everyone sit down together to eat, or do people eat at different times?	Does the teacher use a timer or other tool such as a song to help children wait for snack or during other transitions?
4. Can the child write their name?	Is there a child-sized chair and writing surface at home? How often do adult family members write letters, bills, grocery lists, or other things?	Are the classroom chairs the right size for the children's bodies? Are children offered a variety of writing utensils (markers, pencils, crayons)?
5. Can the child get ready to go outside without assistance?	What sort of shoe fasteners does the child have? Does Mom, Dad, or Grandma put on the child's shoes?	Does the teacher provide a chance to practice zipping a zipper or buttoning a button, other than getting ready to go outside?
6. Can the child identify the top of their head or tell the difference between their left and right?	Are there blocks, beads, toys like LEGOs, or other 3D materials at home that the child plays with?	When playing games with children, does the teacher use vocabulary about directions, size, dimension, and shapes?

Definition of Executive Function: How We Learn

Executive function is the combination of three cognitive processes responsible for planning and learning new things. These processes are generally defined as follows:

Inhibitory control, or ignoring distractions and impulses
Working memory, or remembering and working with information
Cognitive flexibility, or focusing and shifting attention on what's important

In Table 1.1, Item 3, for example, whether children can wait for 30 seconds is related to whether they have ever been asked to wait, such as for dinner at home or a snack at school. When we master our impulses and when we learn new things, we must exert conscious and deliberate effort—and that feeling of effort, or learning being difficult, is EF at work (Floyer-Lea & Matthews, 2004).

Without EF, children can't focus their attention on classroom tasks, remember and work with information or the teachers' instructions about what to do next, or change their behavior and refocus their attention when the situation changes. Without EF, learning is virtually impossible! How EF is involved in learning is the focus of Chapter 3.

Briefly, EF develops rapidly during early childhood with development corresponding with changes in a brain area called the prefrontal cortex, or PFC (Shonkoff & Phillips, 2000). This area of the brain is responsible for imagining the possibility of the future and making plans for that future. A summary of recent research on the brain suggests that in humans, the PFC is impressively connected with several other areas of the brain, including a motor-related area called the cerebellum (Kaufman, 2013).

Definition of Motor Skills: How We Move

Motor skills determine how we move, and are defined as the coordinated and accurate movements of the muscles. For the purposes of this book, such movements include both the conscious and automatic thought processes behind the movements. There are two broad categories of motor skills, each requiring strength, coordination, and perceptual processes:

Fine motor skills, or movements of the small muscles—namely fingers, hands, and mouth
Gross motor skills, or movements of the large muscles of the entire body, including the trunk and limbs

In Table 1.1, Item 4, you might be surprised to realize that children's sitting position is related to their ability to write their name. The developers of the Beery-Buktenica Visuo-motor Integration (VMI) subtest (Beery, Buktenica, & Beery, 2010) emphasize the importance of children's sitting position when using their assessment, which requires children ages 2 and up to use a writing utensil on a sheet of paper (Beery & Beery, 2010). Children who have weak abdominal muscles or who have trouble "crossing the midline" (bringing one hand across the middle of the body) will have more difficulty with a task such as writing that requires sitting upright and controlling their arm, hand, and finger muscles.

Item 5 alludes to constraints that materials or caregivers can place on a child; for example, if children don't wear shoes that tie, they will not have the opportunity to develop that skill. Motor skills are explored more in Chapter 4.

Definition of Spatial Skills:
How We Think About Ourselves and Objects in Space

Spatial skills include a combination of cognitive processes responsible for orienting us and objects in the surrounding environment. Spatial skills are especially important for learning mathematics because quantitative and spatial tasks share many cognitive processes. Here, I emphasize the following processes:

> *Perceptual skills,* or how we perceive spatial information such as location, orientation, and distance
> *Spatial working memory,* or keeping spatial information in mind while we solve a spatial problem
> *Transformational skills,* which we use to imagine changes in the spatial properties of objects or our environments
> *Constructional skills,* which are used when we create from memory or copy a model in 2D or 3D

In Table 1.1, Item 6 shows how spatial information and perceptions apply to both ourselves and to objects in space, and how access to materials and spatial language are important in children's development of spatial skills. Spatial skills are defined and explored in depth in Chapter 5.

SUMMARY

Most teachers realize that the way children behave on the first day of school is not likely to reflect how they will function in the classroom for an entire year. Our initial impressions provide information, but this information is only part of the story and often isn't reliable enough to make long-term decisions about a child's potential.

It's part of the job as professionals working with children to remember that *assessing* whether children are ready for school involves considering their entire complex world—including their home life, previous learning experiences, neighborhood, or community—and *adapting* the classroom context to support their development.

In other words, collecting knowledge and feedback from the child allows teachers to adapt the environment to optimize learning. But deciding what type of information about children should be used to make learning and school readiness decisions is a daunting task. I argue that paying attention to children's foundational cognitive skills can provide teachers with rich information about why certain children may struggle with particular classroom tasks. Because of all the skills that the foundational skills connect to, this type of insight can also help teachers support their students' development in both nonacademic and academic areas.

> **EXERCISE:** As you read this book and are further introduced to the foundational cognitive skills of executive function, motor skills, and spatial skills in Chapters 3–5, try to think about both sides— child and context—of the skill. That is, first imagine the skill as within the child or something a child possesses when you meet them. Then imagine how the early learning environment, including how you interact with your children, may support or constrain the development of that skill.

CHAPTER 2

The Importance of Context in Explaining Young Children's Behavior

---

Understanding Aja—Storyline A

It's been a long day in your classroom. Aja grated on your nerves all day, beginning with morning circle time when she kept trying to play "Duck, Duck, Goose!" and running around the circle. She seems to know just when you are exhausted from staying up half the night with your infant son. Come to think of it, every time you have been especially tired, Aja is particularly disobedient. She must be one of those kids who likes to make things harder for others. "Of course," you think, "when I'm tired, it is more challenging for me to be patient with her as well. But it's not like I'm tired every day—this is just an occasional issue because my baby is teething. With Aja, she is usually like that. It's just who she is."

At the end of Chapter 1, I introduced the idea that contextual factors, such as the materials, resources, and types of interactions that children have at home or in the classroom, contribute to what children can do more than we may realize.

The term *achievement gap* is often used to describe the differences in the achievement scores of children in different SES, race/ethnic, or gender groups, but I prefer the term *opportunity gap*. This latter term points to inequality in the context rather than inherent differences among children. A shift in terminology like this may seem subtle, but it empowers teachers to notice and intervene at the root of the achievement gap problem: in the opportunities and resources that surround children as they develop.

In thinking about children at the lagging end of the opportunity gap, available materials and resources create *constraints* around learning. For example, a child who has never seen crayons before will not likely handle new crayons as well as another child who has a 256-color set.

As another example, if the neighborhood becomes dangerous in the evening, a family may choose to keep their child inside instead of allowing the child to practice riding a bike up and down the driveway. These two issues—not having crayons and living in a dangerous neighborhood—constrain a child's development in fine motor skills and gross motor skills, respectively. (This point is discussed further in Chapter 4.)

While constraints refer to what may be lacking in a child's environment, *affordances* refer to the possibilities that the environment offers, or affords, in the way of a learning opportunity. Note that it doesn't mean what the child is actually learning or doing, but only whether the possibility exists or not. Thinking back to the crayon example: If a child has crayons at home, that environment affords the possibility of using them. But whether the crayons are actually used is up to the child and the family.

In this chapter, I introduce ways to think about how diverse children develop foundational cognitive skills given particular contexts. Not only do children from low-SES backgrounds enjoy less access to learning materials and resources than those from mid- to upper-SES backgrounds, low-SES children experience additional stress that changes the development of their foundational cognitive skills, making it more difficult for children to make long-term, positive choices.

I describe how even though teachers may find it difficult to interact positively with children growing up in poverty, children from low-SES backgrounds stand to benefit the most from positive teacher–child relationships. I suggest how teachers can mitigate negative feelings toward low-SES children and how teachers can understand early childhood classroom environments through the child's experience and better support children.

THEME: Supporting children's school readiness means looking beyond the individual child and to the context for *constraints* and *affordances* of their early learning experiences.

HOW POVERTY AND STRESS IN THE ENVIRONMENT AFFECT YOUNG CHILDREN

The designation of socioeconomic status (SES) is based on multiple characteristics of a child's family, but two of the most commonly used indicators are family income and the education levels of the parents or caregivers. The terms *poor* and *living in poverty* have a specific meaning, which in 2015 was an annual income of $24,036 for a family of four with two children (Jiang, Granja, & Koball, 2017).

Since the late 2010s, the gap between low- and high-SES families in the United States has widened and is now the largest since measurements began in the 1970s. Other economic measures indicate that our country has the greatest wealth imbalance since the Great Depression; specifically, the top 10% of income holders control more than 50% of the nation's wealth (Gamoran, 2015; Noah, 2010).

In 2015, 21% of children under age 6 were in families considered *poor*, and another 24% were in families considered *near-poor*, which is two times the poverty level (so, $48,072 for a family of four). These numbers mean that in 2015, 45% of children were considered low-income (21% + 24%), whereas 55% were not low-income.

Compared to Whites and Asians from middle- and high-SES backgrounds, children of historically disadvantaged racial and ethnic groups have families who earn lower incomes, are more likely to live in areas of concentrated poverty, and have diminished access to high-quality child care and early childhood education (LoCasale-Crouch et al., 2007; Reid & Kagan, 2014). For example, whereas 61% of African American and Hispanic children live in low-income households, 29% and 27% of non-Hispanic Whites and Asians live in low-income households (Jiang et al., 2017).

Living in conditions of poverty or low SES can have negative physical health consequences, because such conditions raise the amount of stress that individuals and families experience. Let's examine in more depth how stress in the environment affects the developing child. In terms of the development of foundational cognitive skills, it is important to consider

- how children adapt to their different environments, especially in low-SES situations; and
- strengths that children from low-SES backgrounds can develop with the encouragement of their teachers.

Adaptations to Living in Conditions of Poverty

Individuals consciously or unconsciously choose strategies that will increase their safety or success in a given environment (Blair & Raver, 2012). In a low-SES environment, limited economic and social resources often make daily life unpredictable. Food, stable housing, and physical well-being may be in question on a regular basis. These stressors contribute to low-SES parents interacting less positively, less responsively, and more punitively with their children compared to parents who are mid- or upper-SES (McConnell, Breitkreuz, & Savage, 2011).

Children use information from the environment to decide whether to control their impulse to take resources when they are available (Kidd, Palmeri, & Aslin, 2013), or to respond to ambiguous situations with aggression. In unstable environments, impulsive responding may actually be adaptive for children, at least in the short term (Blair & Raver, 2012). This is because in unpredictable environments, it is often better to respond quickly to take advantage of an opportunity that may not appear again.

In the classroom, teachers may observe children who are used to unpredictability hoarding their snack or serving themselves more than they can eat. These children may have learned that it is better to eat calories when they are available rather than waiting for a meal that may not appear later. Children's awareness of stimuli is heightened when they grow up with stress, so they may either over- or underreact to noises, minor conflict, or feedback. They may have trouble regulating their negative emotions, such as a child who cries at length over a misplaced coat. Or they may assume the worst about someone's intentions.

For example, a boy may walk too close to a girl sitting at a table, who happens to be kicking her foot under the table and inadvertently kicks the boy. He then believes the girl kicked him on purpose because he is biased to believe that others' accidental or unintentional slights are hostile, known as the *hostile attribution bias* (Dishion & Tipsord, 2011). These responses signal a stress-response system that has adapted to protect the child when the environment—home, neighborhood, or school—is unpredictable and sometimes scary.

Building on Children's Strengths

Scholars of resilience and positive psychology encourage adults working with disadvantaged young children to focus on the positive (Rutter, 2013). That is, instead of only trying to stop children's undesirable behaviors, teachers and other professionals should strive to empower children by identifying and building on the strengths they already have in their behavioral and emotional repertoires (Nickerson & Fishman, 2009).

Applied to activities in the classroom, focusing on the positive also means designing an activity around the skills that children already display. For example, if a child is willing to share materials while working with a partner but not in a group, ensure that they have the chance to work with a partner. If a child can wait for snack for only 3 seconds, use a timer to help them gradually increase to 5 seconds, then 10 seconds, and so on. Remind them of their past successes and focus on their *effort*—not their ability or worth (Dweck, 2006). "You worked so hard!" is healthier feedback than "You're so smart!"

Identifying children's strengths can be a challenge for teachers, especially when children behave in impulsive and reactive ways. Even when teachers can remember that the behaviors may be the result of a child's heightened exposure to stressful living conditions at home, interacting with a child who is having a tantrum creates stress for a teacher (Jennings, 2015).

To learn what individual children need to practice and strengthen their burgeoning foundational cognitive skills, early childhood professionals must develop especially astute skills of observation and the ability to avoid bias in thinking about young children.

BIAS IN TEACHER-CHILD RELATIONSHIPS

Teachers of young children cope with almost constant stimuli, requests, and demands for attention and patience (Feldon, 2007; Jennings, 2015). To deal with the challenge that there is more information in the world than can be thoughtfully processed, humans use different strategies called *heuristics*, or cognitive shorthand.

For example, if it's the beginning of the school year and we are learning names, we might associate children with the first impression they make on us. Maybe we use a trick for remembering names: "Beau is bubbly—boisterous—boy. Callie is quiet—calm—girl." Heuristics are often correct, but not always. Perhaps in the second week of school, you learn that "quiet" Callie's typical behavior is actually extremely extroverted—after she gets comfortable in situations. And Beau's typical state is calm and relaxed, for the same reason!

The Fundamental Attribution Bias

One of the biggest drawbacks that arises from using heuristics to understand children in the early childhood classroom, or any person with whom we interact, is called the *fundamental attribution bias*. This bias means that humans have a tendency to *attribute* another person's mistakes to flaws in that person's character, whereas when we think of our own mistakes, we readily consider our situation and external context.

In Storyline A opening this chapter, the teacher easily realizes that she isn't tired every day. In other words, she considers the context and doesn't think of herself as a "tired person." But in thinking about Aja's behavior, the teacher decides that Aja is a person "who likes to make things harder for others. . . . It is just who she is."

Even though the fundamental attribution bias is a natural cognitive mistake that goes along with being human, guarding against the Storyline A tendency may help prevent incidental conflicts with a given child from clouding the valuable teacher–child relationship.

> **EXERCISE:** Picture a child or family member with whom you had a recent conflict, or Aja from the vignette opening this chapter. Ask:
> » What was going on *in my/the teacher's situation* that may have made the interaction more challenging?

» What was going on *in the other person's/Aja's situation* that may have made the interaction more challenging? (If you don't know, make a note that you are missing information.)
» When is a time that I enjoyed interacting with that person?
» How might I re-create those conditions?

During the early years of school, a positive relationship with their teacher can protect children from difficulties related to challenging behaviors, having low academic skills, or from living in poverty (Hamre & Pianta, 2001). Positive teacher–child relationships are those where the teacher feels close to a particular child, and also has minimal conflict with that child (Hamre, Pianta, Downer, & Mashburn, 2008).

Yet, almost by definition, children who frequently display aggression or anger may be the hardest for a teacher to like—and the easiest to dismiss with an attribution bias: "That's just how this child *is*."

Not all biases are negative. The word "bias" simply means that teachers see children differently than an objective measure of behavior. A positive bias means that the teacher rates a child as having better skills than a more objective direct assessment of the same skill would suggest. A negative bias means that the teacher rates a child as having worse skills than measured with a direct assessment. Large studies show that when teachers rate children, there is often a bias in those ratings that is separate from the child's observable behaviors or skills (Loo & Rapport, 1998; Mashburn, Hamre, Downer, & Pianta, 2006).

Teacher Bias as a Result of Race/Ethnicity and SES

Children's SES and race/ethnicity are two characteristics that are linked to teacher bias (Mason, Gunersel, & Ney, 2014). For example, in a study of 175 early childhood educators in the United States who were told to expect to see challenging behaviors in a classroom video, teachers tended to look longer at the African American children in the video, especially African American boys (Gilliam, Maupin, Reyes, Accavitti, & Shic, 2016). This is significant because the video didn't contain any challenging behaviors, yet teachers' longer gazes revealed their biased expectations for children based on race.

Inaccurate expectations for what individual children can do may lead to teachers providing inappropriate learning experiences. This consequence of teachers' inaccurate perceptions came to light in a study of 20,000 kindergartners. When comparing teacher ratings to individual assessments of children's literacy skills, Ready and Chu (2015) found that teachers perceived students of low SES to have worse skills then they actually did. In an example of a positive bias, teachers perceived students of high SES to have better skills than they did.

What's more, students who were perceived as having worse skills learned less, whereas students perceived as having better skills learned more. This outcome was partially explained after investigating the ability groups into which the children were placed. The researchers found that teachers placed students into ability groups based on their perceptions of their skills, which were partially based on students' SES, thus creating a self-fulfilling prophecy. Teacher bias has real consequences for children.

LEARNING TO SEE HOW CLASSROOM CONTEXTS AFFECT YOUNG CHILDREN

To avoid bias in their expectations for, interactions with, and decisions about children, teachers can use at least three strategies:

- *Realizing that it's normal to misattribute* (mistakenly blame) other people, because we have so little information about them compared to how much we have about ourselves.
- *Working to remember during times of challenge that any person's behavior depends on the situation,* as well as on personal history, tendencies, and traits, and seeking to change the situation if possible.
- *Looking for more information,* such as the teacher in Storyline B (see the end of the chapter), who realizes that Aja has major stress going on at home that may be contributing to her inability to focus during circle time.

Three Categories of Challenging Situations

In early childhood classrooms, children spend the day transitioning through several different types of situations (or settings), each of which has different behavioral expectations. For example, the preschool day may include sitting in a circle with eyes on the teacher, building a tower on the floor with peers, playing alone, moving about the classroom, eating at a table with other children, and sitting near an aide who is explaining a task.

One large study of 3,799 children in 233 Head Start classrooms illuminates the fact that many situations have the potential to challenge children when they begin school (Bulotsky-Shearer, Fantuzzo, & McDermott, 2008). The team drew on data collected within the first 45 days of the school year. Teachers reported all the different learning situations where less than 50% of their children ages 3 to 5 years had trouble meeting behavioral expectations for the situation.

Bulotsky-Shearer and her team's (2008) analysis of the classroom situation data revealed that the different misbehavior-inducing situations fell into three broad categories: (1) structured learning, (2) peer interactions, and (3) teacher interactions.

Challenges in *structured learning* include situations where children must do the following:

- Be appropriately involved in class activities
- Engage in free play/individual choice
- Maintain companions/friends
- Pay attention in class
- Sit during teacher-directed activities
- Take part in games with others
- Work with their hands (as in art)

Challenges in *peer interactions* include situations where children must do the following:

- Behave in the classroom
- Get along with age-mates
- React appropriately to correction
- Show respect for others' belongings
- Stand in line
- Tell the truth

Challenges in *teacher interactions* include situations where children must do the following:

- Answer teacher questions
- Display a generally appropriate manner with the teacher
- Help the teacher with jobs
- Greet the teacher
- Seek teacher help
- Talk to the teacher

> *EXERCISE:* Thinking about a child with whom you have had a hard time forging a positive relationship, circle the behaviors in each of the three categories above that this particular child is still working to develop.

ARE THERE UNSPOKEN EXPECTATIONS IN YOUR CLASSROOM?

I hope that reading about the fundamental attribution bias and research on bias due to SES and race/ethnicity may help teachers develop an awareness of sources of possible bias in their interactions with individual children.

Similarly, in reading the previous section, teachers may more easily recognize how various classroom situations can challenge children. A final strategy is to examine one's own classroom context for areas of confusion or challenge for children.

Unspoken expectations or expectations that change depending on the learning situation can be very difficult for young children to understand. What's more, sometimes teacher expectations are different from what is expected at home or in children's previous classroom settings, which will make it even more challenging for children to succeed.

> *EXERCISE:* Complete Table 2.1 by labeling each behavior (top row, in bold) as "okay," "not okay," or "it depends" for each situation (first column). Think about the unspoken expectations in your classroom or an early childhood classroom that you consider typical.
> » Review your chart. Looking down a single column, do you see a mix of "okay" and "not okay" for a single behavior?
> » Looking at the entire chart, do you see a number of "it depends"?
> » Now, review your chart a final time: In which row do you see the most "not okay" responses, indicating that for that classroom situation, there are few appropriate behaviors?

Table 2.1. Unspoken Expectations Chart

Classroom Situation	Talking to friends	Playing with something in the child's hands	Calling out without raising a hand	Standing up
Building a tower on the floor with peers				
Eating snack with peers				
Moving about the classroom				
Playing with favorite toy				
Sitting in a circle for a book reading				
Sitting next to an aide who is explaining a task				

If you see a mix of "okay" and "not okay" for one behavior, or if you see a number of "it depends," this should alert you to possible challenges for children. Even if you discuss classroom rules and make them as clear as possible, children must use EF (described in the next chapter) to *remember* when certain behaviors are appropriate and when they are not. And even if they can remember those numerous details, children must successfully *change* their behaviors to match the requirements of different situations, all of which may be new for them if they have not been to school before.

You can help children by making the expectations for each situation clear and by allowing children time to practice the skills they need in each learning situation.

SUMMARY

In this chapter, I explained how the stresses of low-income living situations can foster behavior that is adaptive in unpredictable environments, yet maladaptive to the classroom. Children developing skills like remembering classroom expectations and changing their learned or automatic behaviors to conform to new expectations falls under the foundational cognitive skill of *executive function*, the topic of the next chapter.

Even though the behavior of children under stress can be understandably difficult to deal with, teachers can strive to avoid negative biases against children based on their behaviors or group attributes, ask themselves how classroom situations and unclear expectations may contribute to the behavior, and seek to change the situation when possible. In Storyline B, which closes this chapter, instead of dismissing Aja's behavior as representative of her personality, the teacher demonstrates an understanding of the fundamental attribution bias and guards against it in thinking about how to foster a positive relationship with Aja.

Understanding Aja—Storyline B

It's been a long day in your classroom because you were up a couple of times last night with your infant son. Aja had difficulty with the sit-still-and-listen expectations of morning circle time. She wanted to play "Duck, Duck, Goose!" and run around the circle instead. You heard from her grandmother at dropoff that Aja's father missed his parole meeting because the city bus he was taking to get to the meeting broke down, and he's been sent back to prison. "Aja must be trying to distract herself from thinking about home worries," you think. "Even though she's usually high-energy, I can keep up with her when I'm not so tired. I guess it just *feels* like she needs extra attention when I'm exhausted. For the next few weeks, I will try to give us both a break."

Part II

UNDERSTANDING FOUNDATIONAL COGNITIVE SKILLS

CHAPTER 3

How Executive Function Helps Children Learn

You think Jack must have ADHD. During circle time, he constantly gets up from his spot, and even if he manages to sit still for more than a few seconds, he looks around the room, everywhere but at you. His cubby is always a mess, and his shoes are often strewn around the classroom, just waiting for you or one of the assistants to trip.

Jack manages his behavior slightly better during free-choice time, and you have even caught him working for long periods when the blocks or trucks are available. He enjoys most activities where he can use his hands. Still, in those situations, you sometimes have trouble encouraging him to transition to the next activity. He can never seem to remember your carefully worded instructions, which you try to limit to three steps, such as "Finish what you are doing, clean up, and come to the snack table."

Even though Jack is only 4 years old, you hope his parents ask their pediatrician soon about a possible diagnosis. You don't expect kindergarten to be a place where Jack can succeed.

The behaviors in the description of Jack arise because he has underdeveloped executive function and related cognitive skills. *Executive function* is a broad term that emerged from scholarship beginning around 1940 to describe the difficulties that patients with certain neurological conditions exhibit when trying to remember and use information to make plans. In the decades since EF was "discovered," a great deal of scholarship has documented its connection with activity in a brain area called the prefrontal cortex, or PFC (Diamond, 2000), and the dynamic emergence of EF during early childhood, linked with development in the PFC (Zelazo, Carlson, & Kesek, 2008).

In this chapter, I do three things: (1) expand my earlier definition of *executive function* and associated terms, (2) describe common assessments used in research and clinical practice in early childhood, and (3) review the evidence for experiments that attempt to improve EF among young children.

Even for experts who devote years to studying executive function, this is a confusing area of research because of the number of different terms that have been coined to describe EF and its components (Diamond, 2013; Morrison & Grammer, 2016). Yet the implications of underdeveloped executive function in a classroom are straightforward: Children need EF to pay attention and engage in classroom activities. This in turn requires them to control their impulses and remember instructions to carry out the most adaptive behavior for changing situations.

> *THEME:* Executive function includes three different components
> that children need to make good decisions and carry out plans:
> *inhibitory control, working memory,* and *cognitive flexibility.*
> Appropriately assessing executive function in young children is
> a challenge. On the positive side, EF interventions can improve
> individual children's behavior through activities and changes to the
> learning context.

THREE COMPONENTS OF EXECUTIVE FUNCTION

Executive function is not a single skill; rather, it includes multiple skills or components that work together (Miyake, Friedman, Emerson, Witzki, & Howerter, 2000). The research points to three specific components, which I call *inhibitory control, working memory,* and *cognitive flexibility.*

Adele Diamond (2016), an expert on EF in early childhood at the University of British Columbia, calls the three components "core EF skills." Together, they enable higher-order skills such as *reasoning, problem solving,* and *planning* (McClelland, Cameron Ponitz, Messersmith, & Tominey, 2010; Zelazo, Carter, Reznick, & Frye, 1997).

Defining executive function and its components is important because precise definitions can guide early childhood practices, including school-readiness supports and interventions (Bierman, Nix, Greenberg, Blair, & Domitrovich, 2008). Many of the behaviors that kindergarten teachers endorse as most critical for children to have, such as following directions and working independently, rely on EF (Rimm-Kaufman, Pianta, & Cox, 2000). For most children, learning which behaviors are adaptive for a new context like the classroom takes practice that includes trial and error.

Because EF includes three different components, each of those skills must be developed—in other words, they must be allowed opportunities to develop through practice. Likewise, when children like Jack have difficulty related to their EF, it can be because of a problem in one of the three components, or a problem integrating the three and applying them to the sophisticated behaviors needed in the early childhood classroom.

Jack appears to have strong problem-solving and planning skills when it comes to his block play, and he is able to use working memory and cognitive flexibility well when he runs out of space for his planned structure and needs to change his plan. On the other hand, he may be prone to impulsive reactions, such as retaliation, if a peer knocks down a tower that took him 10 minutes to build.

This example illustrates that children can succeed in one EF component but have difficulty with another. Given that EF is involved in executing goals, it's important to consider how to motivate children to align their goals with the goals of their caregivers.

Inhibitory Control

For young children, thriving in most classroom situations means adapting their needs, wishes, and expectations to what their peers and teachers need, wish for, and expect. When needs of the self and the needs of others are aligned, children will experience less conflict between their own wishes and the external constraints. On the other hand, children who need (or feel they need) time to finish their block project, but who are being called to circle time, may experience negative emotions such as frustration or disappointment. They may cope with those emotions by acting out or refusing to join the group.

An adaptive response in that situation requires first inhibiting the impulse to lash out and then ideally choosing a more cooperative response. Inhibitory control is the aspect of EF that is most aligned with regulating one's emotional reactions. *Emotion regulation* represents a vast area of research distinct from EF (Eisenberg & Spinrad, 2004). In this book, I emphasize the cognitive aspects of EF and inhibitory control.

Table 3.1 explains three types of inhibitory control, conceptualized as self-control in the classroom. The first column represents the technical term for the type of self-control, and the second column explains what is being controlled, such as thoughts or behaviors. The third column applies the term in the scenario with Jack and the blocks. The fourth column explains the importance of these three types of self-control for Jack's overall *self-regulation* and success at school. I discuss self-regulation in more depth a little later in this chapter.

Working Memory

In the classroom, children need working memory to remember what they are doing as they do it, and to update their actions when they learn new information, such as when their teacher changes the class's routine for the day because of a visitor.

Two main types of working memory include *phonological working memory*, or working memory for sounds and words; and *spatial working memory*, or working memory for spatial locations (Shah & Miyake, 1996).

Table 3.1. Types of Self-Control in the Block Situation

Type of Self-Control	Definition	Block Situation Example	Importance for Overall Self-Regulation
Cognitive inhibition	Inhibiting *thoughts* and *memories*, i.e., cognitions	Jack is trying not to think about the possibility that a peer will accidentally knock over his tower as he's building it.	If Jack is unable to keep from thinking about this imaginary scenario, he may experience feelings of worry or even anger, and find it difficult to engage productively.
Response inhibition	Preventing or redirecting *behaviors* (e.g., movements or other reactions) that are automatic but not adaptive	When free-choice time ends, Jack represses the urge to throw the blocks across the room and shout, "I'm not ready yet!"	Jack's successful self-regulation of these reactive behaviors keep him from receiving a time-out.
Selective/ focused attention; also known as executive attention	Maintaining one's *attention* to the task at hand	Jack focuses his attention on the block tower for several minutes at a time.	Being able to focus on the block tower gives Jack's body a period of relative calm, which helps him enjoy the rest of his day at school.

I discuss spatial working memory in Chapter 5. For now, *working memory* refers to both types, phonological and spatial.

The "working" part of working memory is really important and distinguishes it from the more familiar concepts of short-term and long-term memory. *Short-term memory* refers to memory of what just happened or was learned, and *long-term memory* refers to memory of what happened some time ago; these types of memory refer mainly to *storage* and *retrieval* of information.

In contrast, working memory refers to "in-the-moment" memory. The term *working* in this case is similar to the idea of a "working draft" or a "work in progress," where stored information is accessed or retrieved, processed, and updated. Thus, yet another term associated with working memory is *updating* (Miyake, Friedman, Rettinger, Shah, & Hegarty, 2001).

Table 3.2 includes terms associated with memory and provides examples from Jack playing with his blocks. Column 1 lists the type of memory, and Column 2 explains what type of information is held in that type of memory. Column 3 provides the technical definition of that type of memory, and Column 4 applies that type of memory to the block scenario.

Table 3.2. Types of Memory in the Block Situation

Type of Memory	Memory for What?	Definition	Block Situation Example
Short-term memory	Things that just happened or information that was just learned	Temporary, limited storage of events, concepts, or other stimuli	Jack remembers his teacher's suggestion to use the pattern of "blue, red, blue, red" in his block tower.
Long-term memory	Things that happened in the past or information that was learned some time ago	More stable (though not necessarily permanent) storage of events or concepts	Jack remembers his favorite school day last week, when he built another block tower.
Phonological working memory, also known as auditory or verbal working memory	Sounds and words	Storing, retrieving, and processing information about sounds and words to guide one's actions in the moment	Jack listens to and carries out his teacher's instructions to come to circle time (e.g., "Stop what you are doing, put away your blocks, and come to the big rug, please!").
Visuospatial working memory	Spatial locations	Storing, retrieving, and processing information about spatial properties or locations to guide one's actions in the moment	Jack visualizes the block tower he built last week, compares that mental image to the one he is building now, and decides to add a moat to this one.

Cognitive Flexibility

Cognitive flexibility refers to when children change their focus of attention or shift their behavior from one activity or set of rules to another. This explains why two other terms for cognitive flexibility are *attentional shifting* and *switching*.

Because cognitive flexibility involves change, it also includes the other two EF components: Changing to a new activity or focus means remembering but *inhibiting* the old activity, and using *working memory* to understand and execute the new (Zelazo, 2015). Because of their immature inhibitory control, young children sometimes have great difficulty switching from one activity to another (Arlin, 1979). Based on this, the average early childhood classrooms, where 22% of time is spent in transition, can be a stressful place (Early et al., 2005).

Not only activities, but a change in rules for behavior involves cognitive flexibility. In Chapter 2, an exercise asked you to reflect on unspoken expectations in different classroom situations, where some behaviors are appropriate in one situation but not another (see Table 2.1).

Children may learn, for example, that they should raise their hand to volunteer during circle time, but then a visitor comes to the classroom who allows children to talk without raising their hands. In this situation, some children may never say a word because they are so used to raising their hands, but other children learn the new rule and soon monopolize the conversation. The second group of children may struggle to switch back to the teacher's expectations when the visitor leaves, however, and continue to freely volunteer their ideas.

Neither group of children has developed the cognitive flexibility that allows them to realize that their teacher has one set of expectations, while the visitor has another. The most adaptive response requires figuring out, for that person or situation, which of many rules apply. But this means drawing on insight and memory skills that most 3- or 4-year-olds have yet to develop.

Development of EF and the Three Components

In the previous example, it is easy to see how the higher-order skill of *reflection*, along with inhibitory control, working memory, and cognitive flexibility, comes in handy in school (Zelazo, 2015). Reflection, along with EF, takes years to emerge in children, however.

The development of EF begins early and is affected by many variables that operate in the realms of biology and neuropsychology, as well as the social environment (Friedman et al., 2008; Resnick, Gottesman, & McGue, 1993; Shonkoff & Phillips, 2000). Early childhood influences are especially strong contributors to the emergence of EF (Blair & Raver, 2015). So far, I have described EF as including three separate components of inhibitory control, working memory, and cognitive flexibility. You may be interested to learn that these components emerge and can be differentiated from one another only at the end of the early childhood period (Huizinga, Dolan, & van der Molen, 2006).

Interestingly, at the beginning of that period, around age 3, the three components all appear to draw on the same cognitive process, leading experts to point out that it makes more sense to talk about overall EF among young children than to overly focus on the three components (Wiebe et al., 2011; Willoughby, Blair, Wirth, & Greenberg, 2012).

For practical purposes, the implications of this scholarship mean that early childhood professionals can support the development of children's EF in a variety of ways, whether with activities that ask children to practice controlling and redirecting their impulses (inhibitory control), remembering and working with information (working memory), or switching rules and flexibly changing their focus (cognitive flexibility).

DEVELOPMENT OF EXECUTIVE FUNCTION IN INFANCY AND CHILDHOOD

If EF is like a growing plant, one of its roots is in a concept taught in many developmental psychology courses, called *temperament*. Teachers of infants may recognize two major aspects of temperament:

Reactivity, or sensitivity to stimuli; some infants are usually easygoing, whereas other infants are bothered by noise, light, and too much activity

Effortful control, which, although it sounds similar to inhibitory control, actually refers to how well children are able to cope with, or regulate, their own reactivity (Calkins, 2007)

Effortful control emerges within the caregiver–child relationship, because caregivers play a significant role in both creating the infant's environment and helping the infant cope with, or modulate, their reactivity (Calkins, 2004; Kopp, 1989). For example, if a baby cries because of a loud party, it is up to the caregiver to take the infant to a quieter spot and to soothe with rocking, shushing, or singing.

When a child is highly reactive to sounds or new events and has trouble regulating that reactivity, child-care settings and school in general will be more difficult for that child. A resource in managing children's reactions to the environment is in how well they can control their attention, also known as *executive attention* (Rothbart, Posner, & Kieras, 2006). Put simply, executive attention refers to where children choose to, or are encouraged to, focus their attention.

Research on executive attention includes tasks similar to Simon Says, where children are supposed to respond to a bear's instructions but not the instructions from an elephant. Laboratory-based studies with children from mostly advantaged sociodemographic backgrounds show that this skill emerges around age 4 (Jones, Rothbart, & Posner, 2003). Only 22% of 3-year-old children could avoid performing the elephant's commands. In contrast, 91% of almost-4-year-olds (46–48 months) could successfully ignore the elephant.

Early childhood professionals can use what they know about a child's temperament, and the power of executive attention, to help children master their reactions and adapt to the classroom environment.

Imagine a 3-year-old girl who becomes upset easily by noises, surprises, or when things don't go her way. At the same time, this child loves to read books and can keep her attention on books for long periods of time. Knowing this, a caregiver can help the child by redirecting her attention during times of stress. For example, if free time often becomes noisy, and you notice the child having increasing difficulty sharing toys with others, you could suggest to the child, "Why don't you go read your favorite book in the story area?"

THE SAME OR DIFFERENT?
EXECUTIVE FUNCTION AND SELF-REGULATION

EF contributes to the development of overall self-regulation, which refers to how children generally cope with and adapt to outside stimuli. (The term *self-regulation* also appears in other fields, to describe how systems—such as ecosystems or social systems—adapt to changing conditions.)

Most scholars in child development, including my colleagues and I, agree that *self-regulation* is a broader and more encompassing term than *EF* (Blair & Raver, 2015; Diamond, 2016; Morrison & Grammer, 2016; Zelazo, 2015). But sometimes the terms *EF* and *self-regulation* are used synonymously, as though they are the same thing. To understand the difference, think about self-regulation as also involving basic, more reactive processes like temperament ("bottom-up"), along with reflective and deliberate EF processes ("top-down").

According to the experts, EF enables a person to develop adaptive regulatory responses to stress and change, but some kind of self-regulation occurs whether or not EF is operating. In other words, all systems and individuals have the capacity for self-regulation, but not all self-regulation involves the deliberate and thoughtful choices that define EF. For example, some infants, when they are overwhelmed with stimuli, may go to sleep. This is a self-regulatory behavior that helps the infant cope with a noisy or busy environment, but infants have not yet developed EF.

My colleagues and I also believe EF operates as part of more general behavioral self-regulation (McClelland, Cameron, Wanless, & Murray, 2007). We have written that children must integrate the separate components of EF and apply them to behavioral responses in the classroom, which we consider *behavioral self-regulation* (McClelland & Cameron, 2012).

When we, as part of an assessment, ask children to touch their toes when told to touch their head, virtually all children demonstrate behavioral self-regulation by attempting to complete the task. But only some children are able to use EF components of working memory and cognitive flexibility to remember the changing rules of the "silly game" and to inhibit the tendency to touch their head when we say "touch your head." Other children smile but clearly forget the instruction to be silly and "do the opposite," because they incorrectly touch their head when we say "touch your head."

Adaptive Self-Regulation Depends on the Context

A helpful compass in navigating this confusing area is thinking back to the idea of what behaviors are *adaptive* for a given context (McClelland et al., 2010). For some children, the same behaviors that are not desirable at school may actually be helpful at home. In Jack's case, his resistance to leaving his block tower detracts from his classroom experience. If he balks and complains when asked to leave the blocks, this behavior may negatively affect his relationship with his teachers and could even mean that he is excluded from the learning opportunities that are offered while he remains with his blocks (Shalaby, 2017).

But what if Jack's home life is full of unpleasant surprises? In that context, a tendency to stay in his room and play with his toys may keep him out of harm's way, in the event of something like a fight among relatives or a violent situation in the surrounding neighborhood.

This framing of adaptive self-regulation as dependent on the context matches Blair and Raver's (2012) research to understand children growing up in low-SES, high-stress environments. As I pointed out in Chapter 2, high-stress living environments are associated with children developing unique stress responses, which mean they are well suited for responding to short-term threats, but not able to develop and plan the long-term strategies (EF) that are emphasized in school settings. Thus, the behaviors that may be adaptive at home may cause trouble at school. Given the significance of the school transition, allowing children to practice EF and doing a good job of assessing this cognitive skill set is a vital part of supporting it.

Self-Talk Supports Self-Regulation

In school-readiness terms, children need opportunities to practice and develop those cognitive and behavioral skills that will allow them to make choices that are healthy in their different environments. Because children rely on language when their EF is emerging, encouraging *self-talk* may help support their making adaptive choices (Winsler, Diaz, Atencio, McCarthy, & Adams Chabay, 2000).

Also known as *inner speech* or *private speech*, self-talk means speaking the situation's rules or plans aloud. Self-talk can be a helpful reminder, especially when children need to demonstrate self-control (Manfra, Davis, Ducenne, & Winsler, 2014).

Going back to our example, Jack needs an external reminder to use EF to remember that although it's appropriate to work for a long time on his blocks at home, at school he must be ready to switch activities when the rest of class is changing. The teachers might work with Jack on a short song or jingle, such as "At school, I'm Super Switch!"

Exercise: Think about a child who has trouble with a classroom rule, perhaps at transition time. Is there a short jingle you could teach them to remember the rule?

ASSESSING EXECUTIVE FUNCTION IN EARLY CHILDHOOD

There is no single best way to assess EF in early childhood, and no single measure provides unequivocal information about children's potential to learn new rules, remember and process information, and control themselves in the classroom. In this section, I use the terms *instrument* and *tool* interchangeably, to refer to different ways of assessing children's EF. Considerations for early childhood professionals who would like to select an assessment of EF for school-readiness purposes include

- the existence of norming data for the tool,
- the tool's validity and ecological appropriateness, and
- access and practicality.

I end this section by describing my own contribution to this area: the Head-Toes-Knees-Shoulders (HTKS) task.

Do Norming Data Exist?

Normative data, or *norms* for short, mean that the tool has been administered to a large group of children with different background characteristics, taking into account race and ethnicity, SES, gender, and, in some cases, disability status. Researchers then calculate the average scores for different subgroups based on age and sociodemographic variables.

In early childhood, the most powerful differentiators of children's performance tend to be age and SES, so a tool that shows race/ethnic differences is probably biased. This is because researchers have determined that SES—not race or ethnicity—is responsible for most differences in early development.

The existence of norms makes it possible, and appropriate, to assess children with a particular instrument and then compare their scores to the expected score for the same subgroup of children with their characteristics (for example, a middle-SES, 6-year-old girl without disabilities).

For school-readiness purposes, especially a high-stakes decision such as whether a child should begin formal schooling, having norming data for an instrument is critical. Unfortunately, tools developed by researchers often lack norming information that would enable their widespread use. This is because such tools are often developed for a single research study, most of which include what are known as *convenience samples*, rather than a norming sample.

Convenience samples are exactly what they sound like: participants whom it was relatively easy, and economical, for the researcher to involve in the study. In contrast, tools developed for practitioners and sold by publishers usually have norms. Having norms is preferable, but is not the only criterion involved in choosing a measure.

Validity and Ecological Appropriateness

Validity means that the tool is truly measuring EF or one of its components—and not something else, like motor skills or vocabulary. Ecological appropriateness means the measure can be administered in a realistic setting, or *ecology*, where it's important for the child to exhibit adaptive inhibitory control, working memory, or cognitive flexibility (Morrison & Grammer, 2016).

Lending complexity to this issue are the many formats of EF measures, such as the following:

Direct assessments administered on a computer or in person, and that require fine motor, gross motor, or verbal responses
Observer reports where parents or teachers answer questions based on their observations and relationship with the child over time
Assessor reports where the person who gives a direct assessment describes how the child attended and behaved during the assessment
Recorded or research-monitored naturalistic observations of children in a laboratory, home, or classroom

All these task-format differences contribute to differences in the way children respond. Along with individual differences in children's EF at the time of assessment, this leads to relatively low correspondence—known statistically as *correlation*—among different EF measures (McClelland & Cameron, 2012).

Because EF changes so much in the years from age 3 to 5, many tools exhibit the problem of *floor effects*, where children are not able to perform any items correctly, or the reverse problem of *ceiling effects*, where they perform all the items correctly. When either a floor or ceiling effect is present, the tool does not provide valid information about the child's EF, other than that their EF level is out of reach of that particular tool (Willoughby, Wirth, & Blair, 2011).

Stephanie Carlson (2005) of the University of Minnesota recommends that professionals who wish to use an EF measure make a decision based on the age of children being assessed. She also suggests deciding whether the goal is capturing differences among children or comparing one child's score to a group standard, as I discussed in relation to norms in the previous section.

Even if a professional identifies a goal, there are possible difficulties with any given tool, which affect ecological appropriateness or validity. For example, the Teaching Strategies (TS) GOLD is a teacher-report tool advertised to assess multiple domains of children's school readiness, including items reflecting EF in the classroom. However, research conducted at the University of Virginia shows that teachers' ratings did not distinguish among individual children as well as direct assessments of children's inhibitory control did (Williford, Downer, & Hamre, 2013).

Teacher ratings of preschoolers' cognitive skills also did not correspond very strongly with the direct assessments. The researchers concluded, "TS GOLD is more influenced by teacher characteristics than direct assessments. This is problematic, given that these measures are intended to assess skill differences between children" (Williford et al., 2013, p. 11).

This study shows one of the more important considerations when trying to validly assess EF, or any school readiness skill, among young children: Does the tool capture unique information about the child in the target skill area, or does it reflect something else, such as another skill altogether or a bias on the part of the person giving the ratings (see also Chapter 2)?

Given the possibility of rater bias, plus documented low correspondence among direct assessments of EF, experts often suggest that this skill should be assessed with multiple tools. This raises the third criterion of access and practicality.

Access and Practicality

Access refers to whether a tool is available and to whom. Some tools used to measure EF must be purchased, require credentials to administer, or both. Though there are good reasons for limiting access based on education or intended use (for example, research versus school-readiness assessment), barriers can be frustrating for early childhood programs or schools.

Practicality is a related issue: A tool may be readily available, but may take too much time to administer to individual children. Similarly, some tools require special equipment, such as a laptop or custom-designed manipulatives, which may be unrealistic for an underfunded early childhood program.

Table 3.3 presents several tools to measure EF and self-regulated behavior in early childhood, organized by whether they are a direct assessment, observer report, or observation in a naturalistic setting. The list in this table is not exhaustive and includes only tools with which I have experience in either their current or previous versions.

Another category of tool, which I have not personally used, is a battery of multiple tasks that are combined into a single composite. A report from scholars at the Educational Testing Service describes three EF batteries with strong evidence for use in early childhood (Ackerman & Friedman-Krauss, 2017).

Table 3.3. Three Types of Research-Based EF Assessments

Name of Tool	Citation	Ages	Cost and Access
DIRECT ASSESSMENT			
Head-Toes-Knees-Shoulders (HTKS)	(Cameron Ponitz, McClelland, Matthews, & Morrison, 2009; McClelland et al., 2014)	4–8	Free for research, no materials needed
Minnesota EF Scale (MEFS), based on the Dimensional Change Card Sort (DCCS)	(Carlson & Harrod, 2013)	2–7	Costs about $8 per child to school district, requires special materials
OBSERVER-REPORT			
Child Behavior Rating Scale (CBRS)—classroom self-regulation subscale	(Bronson, 1994)	3–8	Free upon request
Social Skills Improvement System (SSIS)	(Gresham & Elliott, 2008)	3–18	$700 for basic kit, plus forms; administering requires a master's degree and/or training in assessment
NATURALISTIC OBSERVATION			
Individualized Classroom Assessment Scoring System (inCLASS)—Task engagement domain	(Downer, Booren, Lima, Luckner, & Pianta, 2011)	Pre-K and kindergarten	$2,000, includes 2-day training and 1-year access to video library

THE STORY OF AN EF ASSESSMENT: THE HTKS

My colleague Megan McClelland and I have been studying a direct assessment called the Head-Toes-Knees-Shoulders (HTKS) since 2003 (Cameron Ponitz et al., 2008; McClelland, Cameron, Connor, et al., 2007). I created the HTKS as a graduate student at the University of Michigan, based on my advisor Fred Morrison's reports of a presentation at the Society for Research in Child Development in 2001. Dr. McClelland's and my first papers came out in 2007, which shows the time lag associated with work to develop new school-readiness tools!

The HTKS is a game-like task that asks children to "do the opposite" by touching their head when told to touch their toes, and vice versa. If children perform at a certain level, they move to a more challenging level that adds more rules ("touch your knees when I say to touch your shoulders"), and finally, they can move to a level that switches the rules ("touch your head when I say to touch your knees").

The HTKS is very similar to, albeit more formal than, games like Simon Says and Red Light, Green Light. And not by accident: The first version of the HTKS, called Head-to-Toes, was based on a task called Head-Feet (McCabe, Rebello-Britto, Hernandez, & Brooks-Gunn, 2004). McCabe et al. strove to develop an instrument that would be fun for children and could be administered in diverse settings, including at home and in early childhood classroom environments.

Other scholars, including Fred Morrison and Carol Connor, as well as Angeline Lillard, also contributed to the most recent English version of the HTKS, which demonstrates individual variability and predicts achievement among children ages 4 to 8 years old (McClelland et al., 2014). The HTKS has been translated into more than 20 languages by international researchers throughout Europe. It is also used in Australia and in countries in Africa, Asia, and South America.

Our work and that of researchers across the world demonstrates that children who perform well on the HTKS have higher scores on separate tasks tapping the three components of EF, earn better ratings from teachers on behaviors such as managing materials and working independently, and achieve at higher levels on direct assessments of mathematics, literacy, and vocabulary.

Like any tool, the HTKS is not perfect; it does not yet have norms, which makes it difficult for us to recommend the tool for non-research purposes. The process of designing a study to collect norming data is under way.

REVIEW OF RESEARCH TO IMPROVE EXECUTIVE FUNCTION

In Chapters 6, 7, and 8, I explore the role of EF for nonacademic and academic areas of school readiness. Based on the many, and increasing, number of academic and social outcomes supported by adaptive EF, there have been many attempts to improve children's EF or one of the three components. Summaries of the research indicate that under certain conditions, it is possible to strengthen children's EF (Diamond & Lee, 2011; Rapport, Orban, Kofler, & Friedman, 2013). It is not always easy or straightforward to do, however.

In this section, I describe two major ways researchers have tried to help children develop EF: child-focused interventions and context-based interventions. These categories reflect the main targets of change as being within the child (child-focused) or outside them (context-focused).

Child-Focused Interventions

Child-focused interventions engage individual children in specific activities, administered either in groups or individually. When properly administered, these interventions, also referred to as behavior-based interventions, aim to give children time to practice their EF or the individual components of inhibitory control, working memory, or cognitive flexibility.

In their review of behavior-based interventions, plus curricula targeting EF, Diamond and Lee (2011) found that programs that most successfully improved children's EF involved repeated exposure (known as *dose*) to activities that also increased in difficulty.

Keeping the challenge level high is important because EF, by definition, involves conscious, deliberate decisions. When children become too practiced at something, they can do it automatically—which is good, but it means that the activity no longer requires EF for that child.

Also, the children for whom these programs may work best are those who start with the lowest skill levels (Tominey & McClelland, 2011). For example, Tominey and McClelland administered several whole-group, "circle time games" in half-hour sessions that required children to watch, listen, and control or redirect their body movements and voices when the teacher used visual cues (like color cards), props (like a conductor's baton), or music.

Children in the treatment group who began with the lowest levels of EF improved after 8 weeks of twice-weekly sessions, compared to children in the control group.

Though it is clear that children's EF can be improved with targeted activities, two concerns cloud the promise of behavior-based approaches. The first issue is *transfer*, which is whether improvements in the intervention

WHAT ABOUT COMPUTER GAMES? DO THEY HELP EF?

Growing attention to EF in early childhood has come with efforts to develop games that can be delivered digitally, on a laptop, tablet, or other mobile device. Among young children, there is very little evidence that digital games work to improve EF (Diamond, 2012). Among slightly older children, ages 8 and up, digital training programs called Cogmed improve the EF component that is targeted, whether working memory or cognitive flexibility. However, many research and commercial interventions to support children diagnosed with ADHD targeted short-term memory, not working memory, and had no effects on EF (Rapport et al., 2013).

Another consideration with regard to digital games is the overall amount of exposure to screens that young children experience. The American Academy of Pediatrics (AAP; 2016) recommends that children between ages 2 and 5 be limited to 1 hour of screen time per day, which parents or caregivers should view with children. For children older than 6, the AAP cautions that screen time not replace other activities needed for healthy development, such as positive social interaction, exercise, and sleep.

activities translates into improvements in other areas where more adaptive EF is desired, such as the classroom.

Another concern is *sustainability*, or whether improvements "stick" versus disappear over weeks or months following the intervention—a long-standing issue in education-based work. These two issues allude to the broader problem of targeting only the child, when the science has established that EF emerges within and depends upon supports in a young child's environment. That is why context-based interventions are important, administered alongside or instead of behavior-based interventions.

Context-Based Interventions

Context-based interventions aim to change the surrounding context of the home and classroom, including relationships in those spaces and the interactions that caregivers have with children. I define context-based interventions broadly to include EF-supporting features of the classroom setting and research-developed teacher training programs that focus on classroom organization and management, as well as curricula that have been associated with EF improvements.

Both correlational and experimental research shows what early childhood professionals intuit: Organized and predictable classroom environments support children's internalization of rules and ability to regulate their emotions, thoughts, and behaviors (Cameron & Morrison, 2011; Morris, Millenky, Raver, & Jones, 2014).

For example, in my own research, I asked whether the time that teachers spent orienting children to upcoming activities was associated with several child outcomes, including HTKS performance. Examples of teacher orienting included explanations of center activities and instructions for transitions, such as "When I close the book, I would like you to go to the lunch area and wash your hands."

Orienting and similar proactive organizational activities are examples of EF-supporting general classroom practice. They provide children with appropriate external structure that allows them to predict what will happen next, and to choose behaviors that work well within that structure. Predictable environments mean that children don't have to spend their cognitive energy wondering or worrying, and can focus on learning instead (Curby, Brock, & Hamre, 2013). In my study, which included 140 3- to 5-year-olds from 41 classrooms, I found that children whose teachers spent relatively more time orienting made greater gains on the first part of the HTKS from the beginning to the end of the preschool year (Cameron & Morrison, 2011).

Though modest in statistical terms, these findings match results from large-scale experimental designs, where classrooms and teachers are randomly assigned to either a group that receives support in organization and management or a group that does not. For example, the Chicago School Readiness Project trained one group of randomly assigned Head Start teachers in proactive and redirective behavior management techniques, and compared EF assessments from their children with those of preschoolers in classrooms whose teachers received no support (Raver et al., 2011). Analyses showed that children's EF and self-regulated behaviors improved from fall to spring when their teachers received training in behavior management.

SUMMARY

Executive function fosters children's healthy development and school readiness, and includes three different processes—inhibitory control, working memory, and cognitive flexibility—that are distinct by the end of the early childhood period. Children living in low-income households are more likely to experience the kind of environmental stress that prevents adaptive EF from developing, however.

Children need safe, organized, and predictable environments to be able to practice their EF skills, which can be assessed with direct assessments, observer reports, or naturalistic observations. Appropriate ways for children to practice EF in early childhood involve activities that use motor skills, which I explore in the next chapter.

What About Jack?

After reading about "Red Light, Purple Light" circle time games (Tominey & McClelland, 2011), you incorporate a song to begin and end each circle time activity. The children learn hand motions for each part of the song and watch one another for clues about which hand motion is coming next. You decide that even though the song helps, Jack needs even more support during whole-group activities, because you've noticed he is easily distracted by the other children around him. You invite him near the front of the group and ask your assistant teacher to sit near him.

To encourage Jack to keep his shoes and other materials tidy, you place a picture of his favorite pair of shoes on the bottom of his cubby, along with a picture of his backpack. You also make sure to ask Jack if he slept well last night and ate breakfast. On days when the answer is no, you provide an early snack and try to spend more one-on-one-time with Jack.

Now that you are feeling more hopeful about Jack in a classroom setting, you're eager to pass along what you have learned to Jack's kindergarten teacher, when that time comes.

CHAPTER 4

Motor Skills in Early Childhood

One of the reasons Jack enjoys playing with the blocks so much is that he doesn't have any toys like them at home. In fact, he doesn't have any age-appropriate toys or books that aren't broken or worn out. Happily, the blocks at school are brightly colored and come in many shapes and sizes.

Jack picks up a log-shaped piece and places it carefully next to two others that he is arranging into a moat for his castle tower. To build the tower, he stacks cubes one on top of the other. He builds high enough that he decides to stand up, the better to carefully place the ones at the top.

Suddenly, Alicia, who is one of the clumsiest children in the classroom, walks too close. She stumbles and bumps into Jack's tower, knocking the cubes all around. You look up, ready for an explosion: Jack dislikes when anyone else touches the blocks when he is building, and he's complained about Alicia "bumping me" while he's playing several times this month.

In domains of school readiness, including the Head Start framework described in Chapter 1, Alicia is having difficulty in the domain of Perceptual, Motor, and Physical Development. Motor skills are situated in this domain. On the one hand, this makes sense, because motor skills have to do with movement and are used when we exercise. On the other hand, this categorization obscures the fact that motor skills are intimately connected with children's cognitive development, with this connection starting in infancy and continuing through the school years (Davis, Pitchford, & Limback, 2011).

In this chapter, I define motor skills (*fine motor* and *gross motor*), including contributing skills; review motor development; and describe common motor skills assessments used in research and clinical practice in early childhood. I also describe interventions to improve motor skills. I return to the idea of *constraints* and *affordances*, introduced in Chapter 2, and contextual factors, including family factors, that can constrain children's ability to exercise and acquire motor competence.

> **THEME:** Motor skills are the first learning experience we have as humans, and so they set the stage for later learning of all types. This helps explain why motor skills are linked to so many different skills that children need in school.

DEFINITION OF MOTOR SKILLS

In nontechnical circles, the word *motor* is usually associated with movement through space. As for EF, this area of research also includes some debate about basic definitions, such as what the term *motor* means.

On the one hand are experts from traditions like kinesiology, who propose that the word *motor* refers not just to the movements of our bodies and limbs in space, but also to the cognitive processes that make those movements possible (Burton & Rodgerson, 2001). On the other hand, definitions such as the one suggested by the American Occupational Therapy Association (AOTA; 2014) limit motor skills to what can be seen—specifically, "observable elements of action that have an implicit functional purpose" (American Occupational Therapy Association, 2014, p. S25).

Like kinesiologists, I use the term *motor* broadly, with underlying cognitive processes implied (Cameron, Cottone, Murrah, & Grissmer, 2016). I hope that when you finish reading this chapter, you'll appreciate the extent to which the physical movements that support school readiness also reflect children's perceptual and cognitive skills. Keeping in mind the importance of context (see Chapter 2), motor skills emerge within a rich world that includes the individual child, family, school, and community (Bronfenbrenner & Morris, 2006). Variables at each of these levels can limit or enable children to add certain motor skills to their repertoire.

Another message in this chapter that I hope to leave you with is an appreciation of how often early childhood classrooms expect children to engage in learning activities that require specific movements. In other words, "doing school" requires basic competence with particular motor skills. Next, I briefly define gross and fine motor skills, and discuss *qualities* such as strength and *processes* such as motor planning that contribute to children's motor skills. Although the list of qualities and processes in this chapter is not exhaustive, I describe several concepts that are especially relevant for learning in school.

Gross Motor Skills

Gross motor skills refer to the coordinated movements and other processes of the large muscles of the body, including the core-stabilizing muscles of the torso. The components that make up gross motor competence vary depending on the source.

In one study of 233 7- and 8-year-olds with mild intellectual disability, gross motor skill categories included speed and agility, coordination, balance, and strength (Wuang, Wang, Huang, & Su, 2008). And a website based in Australia lists 12 skills that it calls "building blocks necessary to develop gross motor skills" (Kid Sense Child Development Corporation, 2017). With a few exceptions (like balance), these skills and building blocks are also relevant for fine motor skills.

Fine Motor Skills

Fine motor skills refer to coordinated movements and processes of the "small" muscles of the wrists, hands, fingers, feet, and toes. As with gross motor skills, attempts to identify a core set of fine motor skills result in long lists of skills that mainly reflect the numerous specific tasks that we perform with fine motor muscles (American Occupational Therapy Association, 2014).

Years ago, one group of researchers listed skills such as speed, steadiness, and skill at assembling materials (Seashore, Buxton, & McCollom, 1940). Adults may be surprised to realize how much and how often children must rely on their fine motor skills to navigate the early childhood classroom (Marr, Cermak, Cohn, & Henderson, 2003).

Contributors to Motor Skills

Many contributors to motor skills exist. In this section, I describe the following qualities and processes that contribute to motor skills and highlight their relevance for school readiness:

- Strength and precision
- Balance, body awareness, and coordination
- Speed, sequencing, and motor planning

Strength and precision. One of the most familiar concepts related to motor skill and physical prowess in general is probably *strength*, or how much force muscles exert or can withstand. Core strength as well as limb muscle strength contribute to gross motor skill, whereas finger, wrist, and hand strength contribute to fine motor skill.

Precision means being able to perform a task accurately, whether it is lining up directly behind a friend, placing beads on a string, or connecting the dots in a coloring book. Precision and strength are interrelated. For example, holding a pencil or other writing utensil requires adequate strength to keep the implement steady while forming letters precisely. Certain grips make it easier for preschool-age children to write (Burton & Dancisak, 2000).

Balance, body awareness, and coordination. *Balance* means being able to keep one's entire body in a certain, desired position in space. Balance requires body awareness; the technical term is *proprioception*, a perceptual skill indicating awareness of one's body in space based on subconscious feedback from our muscles and joints. When Alicia bumped into Jack's tower, it was because she lost track of the sense of her own body in space, which caused her to lose her balance.

Types of Fine Motor Tasks in Preschool and Kindergarten

Deborah Marr, an occupational therapist, and her colleagues (2003) conducted a widely cited observational study of 10 Head Start and 10 kindergarten classrooms. They selected two representative children from each classroom, and observed every activity in which those two children engaged for the entire school day. They found that children used their fine motor skills in both academic and nonacademic tasks.

Examples of *nonacademic* tasks that required fine motor skills included dressing and hygiene, eating, participating in arts and manipulative activities, and playing at centers such as sand tables. Examples of *academic* tasks that required fine motor skills included writing and anything with a writing or coloring tool; book reading where children were handling the book; and cutting, gluing, or otherwise working manually with an academic worksheet.

Marr et al. (2003) found that children in Head Start spent, on average, 37% of their time in some type of fine motor activity, and this percentage of time increased to 46% for kindergarten children. Most of the fine motor time in Head Start was nonacademic (35%) versus academic (2%), whereas kindergarten children's time was divided almost equally between nonacademic (26%) and academic tasks (20%).

One of the primary concerns among children with developmental coordination disorder (DCD) is balance. DCD used to be referred to as "clumsy child syndrome" and affects around 6% of children ages 5 to 11 (Piek et al., 2004). Research suggests that children with DCD do not use proprioceptive (body awareness) cues the same way as do children without the diagnosis (Dewey & Wilson, 2001). Another diagnosis that implicates motor skills and development is Down syndrome, also known as Trisomy 21.

Body awareness depends on the vestibular sense, which children use to orient their head and entire body in space. An occupational therapist helped me understand the vestibular sense as your sense of knowing that you are moving in a car, even if your eyes are closed. Experts consider proprioception and vestibular senses as sensory rather than motor functions, but keeping one's balance while moving about the classroom or playground depends on both these concepts and so I include them (American Occupational Therapy Association, 2014).

Coordination is the "ability to integrate multiple movements into efficient movement" (Kid Sense Child Development Corporation, 2017). This necessitates good timing among the different movements or processes of the large muscles involved in a gross motor action.

MUSCLE TONE IN CHILDREN WITH DOWN SYNDROME

One of the most common characteristics of children with Down syndrome is weak muscle tone, called hypotonia. This concept is not straightforward but refers to the amount of resistance that ligaments and muscles exert in relation to a force (Latash, Wood, & Ulrich, 2008).

Another way to think about the muscles of a person with low tone is that they are more relaxed than is typical. Low tone is thought to contribute to children with Down syndrome experiencing delayed early motor milestones such as rolling over, crawling, and walking, compared with children without the diagnosis.

To explain this difference to young children, a teacher might say something like, "Evan's muscles have to work harder than yours to do the same work. That is why it takes him longer to do some things in the classroom."

A coordination skill known colloquially as *crossing the midline* refers to children's ability to perform tasks on the opposite side of their body with their hands and limbs. Technically known as *bilateral* (two-sided) *integration*, crossing the midline requires reaching, stepping, or looking across the imaginary vertical line down the center of the body.

One study of nine 4-year-olds showed that it takes longer to perform tasks on the opposite side of the body (Screws, Eason, & Surburg, 1998). Many exercise activities, self-care tasks, and school assignments like sitting at a surface and writing require children to be comfortable with crossing the midline.

Speed, sequencing, and motor planning. There are two types of speed when it comes to motor tasks: how fast children can repeat the same movements and how fast they can repeat a sequence. *Speed of sequencing* of a gross motor task like heel-toe tapping or a fine motor task like touching one's thumb to each finger provides a reliable indicator of children's cognitive and academic skills in the school transition years (Martin, Tigera, Denckla, & Mahone, 2010; Wolff, Gunnoe, & Cohen, 1985).

The planning and spatial sequencing involved in physical movements, called *motor planning* or *praxis*, has led experts to describe motor development as how children learn to learn (Adolph & Berger, 2006; Willingham, 1998). In other words, children discover how learning works through attempting, failing, and finally mastering motor tasks. Given how important motor tasks are for learning in general, early childhood professionals may find it helpful to consider how children who struggle with motor tasks may experience school.

Body Awareness Develops During Early Childhood

Though teachers may notice something as basic as balance if a child falls frequently, you may find it interesting to know that body awareness develops during early childhood, and an undeveloped sense of proprioception helps explain why new walkers tend to veer off their course. One study with 140 children found that body awareness improved the most between ages 5.8 and 7.8 years (Sigmundsson, Whiting, & Loftesnes, 2000). The researchers measured body awareness by first blindfolding children and moving a foot. Children then had to imagine as precisely as they could where their big toe was located, and "match" that location with their hand.

> *Exercise:* Early childhood classrooms can provide opportunities to develop balance in exercises such as walk-a-line or carrying a full spoon. Practicing one's balance also requires one's full attention, so it may be a useful way to address issues like Alicia's and Jack's or to quiet a group of rowdy children. Can you think of one to two activities you could do to help children improve their body awareness, balance, or coordination?

DEVELOPMENT OF MOTOR SKILLS IN INFANCY AND CHILDHOOD

In this section, I highlight two important themes regarding the development of motor skills: first, the role of the early environment in providing *affordances* for movement and, second, how motor and cognitive development go together, a concept called *co-development*.

The Early Environment Affords or Constrains Motor Learning

Motor skills are one of those areas of development that depend crucially on environmental inputs (Roeber, Tober, Bolt, & Pollak, 2012; Scott, 1962). The nationally representative Early Childhood Longitudinal Study of Kindergarten (ECLS-K; 1998–1999) included 50 sets each of identical and fraternal twins, as well as a large number of other children, for a total sample size of more than 20,000. Grissmer and Eiseman (2008) used the data to document how genetics versus environment contributed to motor skills measured at kindergarten entry. They compared the average differences in identical twin pairs, fraternal twin pairs, and a random pair of one identical twin compared to an unrelated child in the data set, who had similar background characteristics.

Figure 4.1 shows the distance or magnitude of difference between children (identical twins, fraternal twins, and unrelated pairs) on three

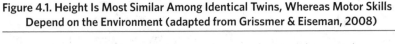

Figure 4.1. Height Is Most Similar Among Identical Twins, Whereas Motor Skills Depend on the Environment (adapted from Grissmer & Eiseman, 2008)

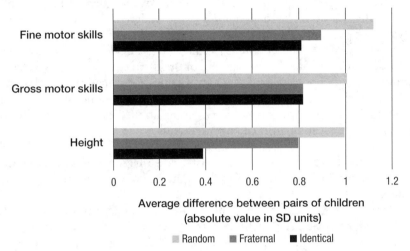

developmental variables assessed at kindergarten entry: height, gross motor skills, and fine motor skills. The units are all in standard deviation (SD) units for that variable, which allows them to be charted on the same scale. In a group of children with the same score on a test or measure, the standard deviation indicates how far one child's score lies from the average score for the group.

Notice how, for the developmental variable of height, identical twins have a small magnitude or short bar, but unrelated pairs of children have a large magnitude or tall bar. This means that genetics contributes a lot to height—because identical twins, who share the same genes, are much less different from unrelated pairs of children when it comes to height.

On the other hand, the sizes of the three bars are more similar for all three groups when it comes to motor skills. This means that the environment contributes more to children's level of motor skills than to their height.

Because children's developing motor skills depend so much on the environment, we would want to know how and which environmental differences contribute to motor skill differences. A follow-up study, also using ECLS-K data, speaks to this question (Potter, Mashburn, & Grissmer, 2012).

Potter et al. (2012) first established that SES differences exist in children's fine motor skills, reporting that children in the bottom fifth of households, in terms of SES, scored about 0.66 of a standard deviation (SD) lower than children in the top fifth of households. Potter et al. then were able to explain 30% of that 0.66 difference—or 0.20 of an SD—with only a few family variables, specifically "involvement with more activities, greater parental educational expectations, and more books in the household" (p. 454).

Even though these variables don't have to do with fine motor skills specifically, they allude to potentially vast underlying differences in the learning opportunities that families with financial and social advantages are able to provide for their children. Families that struggle to make ends meet because of low income, low education, or other stressors may not be able to afford activities and resources, including educational materials and games that allow children to exercise their developing motor skills at home. This study illustrates how the opportunity gap mentioned earlier contributes to gaps in children's foundational cognitive skills.

What is more, families of low-SES children are more likely to live in neighborhoods where playing outside isn't safe; this *constraint* further limits children's learning opportunities to the limited activities that can be pursued indoors.

Similar to the idea of being able to afford a financial purchase, an *affordance* is a possibility of action on an object or in one's environment (see also Chapter 2). If the environment is limited because it is unsafe to explore or because it offers few objects or stimulating learning materials for children to interact with, the affordances in the environment are low. Caregivers can also unknowingly limit environments for children, which has implications not just for their motor skills but for their cognitive skills as well.

Co-Development Among Motor and Cognitive Skills

The concept of co-development means that two skills develop together. Especially in infancy, but with more evidence for early childhood co-development emerging all the time, motor skill acquisition goes together with cognitive achievements.

Karen Adolph is a professor at New York University who asks permission from parents to videotape and code infants while they move about in her customized laboratory. She and her team have documented thousands of attempts by infants to learn to crawl, climb, or walk (Adolph, 2015; Adolph & Berger, 2006). This impressive body of work, which depends on carefully watching the videotapes and counting the various movements that each infant makes, has led Adolph to describe motor learning as "learning to learn." This theory is based on the idea that infants' first learning experiences have to do with movement (Thelen, 2005).

Though to many parents, their infants seem to change almost overnight, the amount of repeated practice that goes into accomplishments like crawling or learning to cruise the furniture is astounding. Throughout the first months of life, infants attempt the same action toward their particular goals thousands of times, with earlier movements creating networks in the brain that are used later for making more refined and nuanced movements. From those experiences, children learn about how the world works, how their bodies work, and what to expect from the environment.

As I described in Chapter 2, caregivers help shape children's early environments, and their interactions connect to both cognitive and motor development. For example, one study using the Early Childhood Longitudinal Study-Birth (ECLS-B) data set showed that when parents exhibited more negative interactions in a parent–child play scenario, children's fine motor skills were lower (Chen, Grimm, Grissmer, & Gregory, 2010). This association played out over time: When parents were more intrusive and controlling at age 2, children's fine motor skills were lower at age 4. This pattern persisted for parent negativity at age 4 and children's fine motor skills at age 5.

Another predictor of low motor skills at age 4 was low cognitive skills at age 2. Unfortunately, children who had low motor skills at age 4 also had lower academic achievement at age 5 (Chen et al., 2010), controlling for their earlier levels of cognitive achievement and parenting interactions.

This study illustrates the complex associations among cognitive and motor development, and environmental factors like parenting, over the early childhood years. Parenting was also related quite specifically to child skills: For example, early positive parenting behaviors were associated with children having better cognitive skills later; negative parenting interactions were associated only with lower levels of fine motor skills, but did not predict children's cognitive skills or achievement.

Going back to the idea of affordances, Chen et al. (2010) noted:

> Intrusiveness, in particular, may disrupt fine motor learning by limiting children's opportunities to practice certain actions. A parent negatively stepping in to prevent a child from completing a task too quickly, too slowly, or "incorrectly," may in fact impede the child from learning to complete the task at all. (p. 22)

These findings are consistent with other research showing the negative effects of parent intrusiveness for young children (Cabrera, Shannon, & Tamis-LeMonda, 2007).

Translated to the early childhood classroom, a child who constantly hears "no" at home may either avoid exploring at school and learn to sit quietly instead, or may show frustration by acting out (Shalaby, 2017). Such children may be deprived of practice in their motor skills, and assessing their skills can help provide targeted support.

ASSESSING MOTOR SKILLS IN EARLY CHILDHOOD

Tables 4.1, 4.2, and 4.3 display several measures of gross motor and fine motor skills in three categories: (4.1) those based on a single or small number of tasks, (4.2) comprehensive test batteries in multiple areas, and (4.3) observer reports of children's motor skills. For most tests, I include sample items to further illustrate the diversity of skills that comprise motor competence. Most fine motor tests include at least one measure of visuo-motor integration, which I consider a spatial skill in this book and discuss at length in Chapter 5.

Brief Direct Assessments

Table 4.1 includes a subtest of perhaps the most widely known test of visuo-motor integration, the Beery-Buktenica VMI (Beery, Buktenica, & Beery, 2010) or the Beery VMI for short. The main subtest on the Beery VMI asks children to copy increasingly complex designs.

Two other related subtests on the Beery VMI are a measure of visual perception where children identify as many exact matches to stimuli in 3 minutes, and the motor coordination subtest, included in Table 4.1, where children trace the same designs that they copy. The motor coordination subtest is meant to be administered after the VMI subtest. The Beery VMI can be given in a group setting such as a classroom, and assesses a more limited set of skills related to fine but not gross motor development.

Also included in Table 4.1 is the revised version of Early Screening Inventory (ESI-R), which consists of a few tasks in three areas: visual-motor/adaptive, language and cognition, and gross motor. The publisher website states that the ESI-R is (1) a broad *sample* of developmental tasks, rather than representing specific accomplishments that indicate academic readiness; and (2) an assessment of *aptitude*, or a child's ability to acquire skills, rather than the child's current level of skill achievement and performance.

The ESI-R fine motor tasks also heavily tap visuo-motor integration because they ask children to copy simple forms such as a circle or square, or copy an examiner's block design using their own building blocks. The item that relies only on fine motor coordination, not visuo-motor integration, asks children to build a tall tower out of several same-size blocks.

Comprehensive Test Batteries

Table 4.2 includes three of most common comprehensive test batteries of motor skills that span early childhood. These assessments involve considerable time, space, and materials to administer, but they are able to provide detailed information on quite a range of motor skills. Without exception, these batteries require special training and/or permission from the publisher to administer, and are costly.

Table 4.1. Two Brief Direct Assessments of Motor Skills

Name of Assessment, Publisher, & Cost	Citation	Ages	Gross Motor Skills, Format, & Example Items	Fine Motor Skills, Format, & Example Items
Beery VMI, motor coordination subtest, Pearson, $149 for complete test kit	(Beery, Buktenica, & Beery, 2010)	2:0–99:11	N/A	Child "traces" the figures from the VMI subtest by connecting provided dots.
Early Screening Inventory-Revised (ESI-R), Pearson, $162 for complete kit	(Meisels, Marsden, Wiske, & Henderson, 2008)	3:0–5:11 years	Balance, hop, skip Gross motor coordination Ability to imitate body positions from visual cues	Build a tower with blocks. Other fine motor items require visuo-spatial skills. See Chapter 5.

Publisher website information about these measures advertises their appropriateness for measuring fine and gross motor skills, but outside research tells a more complicated story. For example, a review of the Bruininks-Oseretsky Test of Motor Proficiency (BOTMP, now known as the BOT™-2), concluded that "The items on the BOTMP do not discriminate between fine motor and gross motor abilities. Rather, the BOTMP is a measure of general motor proficiency" (Wiart & Darrah, 2001, p. 281). The measure has been modified to the updated BOTMP-2 version reported in this table, but it's not clear whether the updated scales are able to distinguish between fine and gross motor skills.

A similar issue exists with the McCarron Assessment of Neuromuscular Development (MAND). A 2017 study by McIntyre and colleagues reviewed available psychometric information, which is quite limited—specifically, original test data included only 39 7-year-olds who were typically developing. Those results have not been replicated with larger samples of children of different ages. The most appropriate use of the test appears to be identifying children with motor impairments.

A very common battery is the second edition of the Movement Assessment Battery for Children (MABC-2). This test claims to assess the same underlying skills (ball skills, manual dexterity, and static balance) at different ages, but uses different tasks that are deemed appropriate for children at a given age. The test items are protected, so descriptions of specific tasks are generally unavailable. The examples shown in Table 4.2 are taken from individual studies by outside researchers.

Table 4.2. Three Comprehensive Test Batteries of Motor Skills

Name of Assessment, Publisher, & Cost	Citation	Ages	Gross Motor Skills, Format, & Example Items	Fine Motor Skills, Format, & Example Items
Bruininks-Oseretsky Test of Motor Proficiency, Second Edition (BOT™-2), Pearson, $900 for complete test kit	(Bruininks & Bruininks, 2005)	4:0– 21:11 years	Bilateral Coordination: tapping foot and finger, jumping jacks Balance: walking on a line, standing on one leg Running Speed and Agility: one-legged side hop Upper-Limb Coordination: throwing ball at target Strength: sit-ups	Fine Motor Precision: cutting out a circle Fine Motor Integration: copying a star Manual Dexterity: stringing blocks
McCarron assessment of neuro-muscular development (MAND), McCarron Dial website, $1945 for complete kit	McCarron, L. (1997)	3.5– 18 years	Five gross motor tasks: finger-nose-finger, grip strength, standing jump, line walking, one-leg balance	Five fine motor tasks: beads in box, bead on rod, nut and bolt, finger tap, rod slide
Movement Assessment Battery for Children (MABC-2) Test, Pearson, $1,050	(Henderson, Sugden, & Barnett, 2007)	3:0– 16:0 for test	Ball skills (examples for ages 11-15: catch a self-thrown ball) Static balance (no examples found)	Manual dexterity (examples for ages 5-6: depositing coins in a box with a slot, placing pegs into holes, threading beads on a lace)

Observer-Report Surveys

Finally, Table 4.3 includes two examples of observer-report surveys of children's motor skills. I included the MABC-2 checklist because it is so widely used. There appear to be differences between teachers' and parents' ratings of children ages 5 to 8 years using the checklist, however (Schoemaker, Niemeijer, Flapper, & Smits-Engelsman, 2012). Misalignment in different

Table 4.3. Two Observer-Report Surveys of Motor Skills

Name of Survey, Publisher, & Cost	Citation	Ages	Format and Example Items
Movement Assessment Battery for Children (MABC)-2 Checklist, Pearson, $1,050	(Henderson et al., 2007)	5:0–12:0 for checklist	30 items assessing movement in two broad categories: • Static/predictable environment: classroom, phys. ed./recreational, and self-care skills • Dynamic/unpredictable environment: ball skills, phys. ed./recreational, and self-care/recreational
Motor Skills Rating Scales (MSRS), upon request to author, free	(Cameron, Chen, et al., 2012)	K–2nd grade	Gross motor: One teacher-reported subscale: body awareness Fine motor: Three teacher-reported subscales: body awareness (primarily gross motor), classroom fine motor, shapes and letters (fine and visuo-motor)

caregivers' perceptions of children's skills is a problem when trying to identify students who might qualify for occupational or physical therapy. For example, the MABC-2 checklist does not identify very precisely those children who have motor impairments at school, so researchers explicitly note that it should not be used as a screener.

The MABC-2 checklist and similar rating scales were designed to identify disabilities determined by performance on specific tasks given by clinicians, such as keeping one's balance while throwing a ball back and forth (Dirksen, De Lussanet, Zentgraf, Slupinski, & Wagner, 2016; Netelenbos, 2005). Meanwhile, teachers' views of children's motor skills depend more on how students function in the classroom, not on how students perform on a clinical task battery that teachers do not see. So, developing a measure of the daily motor requirements of classrooms is a promising and important direction to help early childhood professionals understand motor skills across the range of children in their classroom.

I had the privilege to lead the development of the Motor Skills Rating Scale (MSRS) with a team that included a clinical school psychologist, a special education professional, and a former teacher, in consultation with two occupational therapists (Cameron, Chen, et al., 2012). The entire scale includes 19 items that ask teachers about students' body awareness in the gross motor domain, and about their classroom fine motor skills and facility with shapes and letters in the fine motor domain.

In two separate studies involving a total of 386 diverse students in kindergarten, 1st, and 2nd grade, we found that children who were rated positively on the scales also had better cognitive skills, academic achievement, and social skills.

For example, children who were able to copy shapes and letters also did better on a precision assessment requiring them to stay in between lines when using a writing utensil. In contrast, children who struggled to manage their bodies and objects in the classroom, who were rough with books and other learning resources, were rated by their teachers as having poor social skills and more problem behaviors.

REVIEW OF RESEARCH TO IMPROVE MOTOR SKILLS

It may go without saying that many school-based interventions use activities and exercises in which children move. Yet just because an intervention incorporates movement doesn't automatically mean that motor skills are being targeted on purpose. Perhaps because school does not *explicitly* prepare children to excel in motor skills, research on motor skills interventions is relatively sparse, at least compared with EF interventions.

In this section, I summarize findings from several reviews of interventions on motor skills that seem especially relevant for early childhood. These reviews include the following:

- Two reviews of international research to improve preschool-age children's gross motor skills (Riethmuller, Jones, & Okely, 2009; Veldman, Jones, & Okely, 2016). Of the 17 total studies in these two reviews, nine were based in the United States, three in Australia, two in Greece, and one each in Switzerland, Taiwan, and the United Kingdom.
- A review of interventions with preschoolers diagnosed with a developmental delay (Kirk & Rhodes, 2011).
- A review of interventions using random assignment that were conducted with children diagnosed with developmental coordination disorder (DCD) (Pless & Carlsson, 2000).

Of note, existing work has either focused on gross motor skills or involved only children with a developmental delay. These limitations mean that much more work remains for researchers to understand how to go about improving fine motor skills, or effective motor skills interventions for typically developing children.

Even so, as the evidence grows for motor skills supporting cognitive and academic performance in typically developing children (see especially Chapter 6), interventions to improve motor skills in nonclinical populations may become more popular. Therefore, it makes sense to learn from the base of research that does exist, even if it is somewhat limited. The three conclusions I discuss next are derived from one of the reviews (Pless & Carlsson, 2000), and are relevant to thinking about supporting motor skills in early childhood.

Teaching Specific Tasks Is Better Than General Training

Looking across the reviews, it's appropriate to conclude that children's motor skills do get better with deliberate support. Interventions that taught children specific tasks were more successful, compared to trying to improve their general balance and coordination or their ability to integrate sensory information. This is consistent with research that dismisses general perceptual-motor approaches to improve cognitive skills (Hammill, Goodman, & Wiederholt, 1974), which enjoyed brief popularity in the 1960s (Kephart, 1964).

Children Should Practice Skills Several Times per Week

Second, interventions are more successful when the "dose" is relatively high: specifically, when children experience the activities three to five times per week, compared to less often. For example, Kirk and Rhodes (2011) found that among children with DCD, an average of 13 weeks of intervention occurring one to four times per week successfully improved gross motor skills such as running, jumping, throwing, and catching.

In other words, the "practice makes perfect" adage is true for motor skills interventions; in research circles, this concept is referred to as "distributed practice." Thinking about how the brain works, the skills that are practiced or distributed over time become easier, or more automatic (Floyer-Lea & Matthews, 2004). And more-frequent practice means that automation happens sooner.

Small-Group and Home Programs Work Better than One-on-One

Third, Pless and Carlsson (2000) found that small-group and home programs were more successful than one-on-one interventions. In general, however, interventions also worked better for children older than 6 years, compared with attempts to help the motor skills of 3- to 5-year-olds. The researchers also noted that certain small-group activities may not be appropriate for young children.

All authors suggested on the basis of their reviews that interventions involve not only school professionals, but parents too, to help create more consistency and opportunities to practice motor skills across children's different settings. This makes sense, given that children use their motor skills during all waking hours—not just when they are at school.

SUMMARY

Motor skills involve many processes that allow children to move about and interact with objects in their environment. Early childhood classrooms are full of motor tasks, especially fine motor tasks. These requirements mean that school is easier for some children than others, depending on their prior experiences and achievements in motor development. In early childhood, motor skill successes such as going to the bathroom alone, tying shoes, learning to cut with scissors, and writing take lots of practice.

As in the situation with Alicia knocking over Jack's blocks, teachers may not notice or feel concerned about a child's motor skills unless something goes wrong. Indeed, much of the literature on motor development involves children with disabilities or other conditions that significantly impair their motor functioning. Yet differences in the motor skills of typically developing children are substantial and linked to SES and family interaction variables.

Assessing motor skills for all children is a good idea, but batteries can be costly and teachers may find it difficult to decide which skill or skills they should assess. Teachers may consider using a brief rating scale that asks about motor skills and involving their school's occupational therapist if some children have more obvious trouble with body awareness, using materials, or performing basic self-care activities such as putting on shoes or clothes that other children in the classroom have mastered. Finally, interventions to improve motor skills are promising, but more research is needed. Interventions where children have the chance to practice the same sets of tasks at least a few times per week will be more successful than general movement exercises done less regularly.

Jack and Alicia

After Alicia knocks over Jack's tower, she quickly offers to help him rebuild it. He says, "No!" but he seems to realize she didn't do it on purpose. You decide to ask them to help each other during transitions. Each day, Jack carries Alicia's belongings when she moves about the classroom, and in return, Alicia helps Jack clean up the blocks area.

Alicia's calm and quiet presence seems to help Jack focus on clean-up, and she isn't as clumsy when she's not worried about making Jack angry. The two of them eventually become friends and sit together during circle time and snack. You are proud of yourself—and the children—for finding a solution to what seemed like an unsolvable problem.

CHAPTER 5

Spatial Skills
Important but off the Radar

This week, Jack has seemed like a different child. You introduced the game Animal Matching, which uses a grid of 3-inch-by-3-inch cards turned facedown. Children look for pairs of cards with a mother and baby animal of the same species. The goal is to collect as many matched pairs as possible. At each turn, players flip over any two cards; if they find a match, they may flip over two more. If they select two unmatched animals, they have to wait for their next turn, and all cards are again placed facedown. To win, a player must remember where the animals are so that when its match is revealed by another child, the player can flip over the target and its match.

Jack is easily the best in the class at the Animal Matching game, so good that you have him move around during the game, because changing his seat should make it harder for him to remember where matches are—in theory. Even when his seat constantly changes, he usually wins the game.

The reward for winning at Animal Matching is being the first child to choose a spot during free-choice time. Jack usually chooses the blocks area, but this week he asked you to come and build a tower with him. This never happens—you didn't even think that Jack liked you! You decide to find a picture of an intricate castle that you remember came with the new blocks kit. Together, you and Jack try to make one just like it. You put him in charge, and are impressed at all the spatial language he uses and understands: "Put that round one between the square ones," "Let's build a high tower next to where the moat will be," "Put that long block behind the wall."

These games help you realize that Jack's spatial skills are quite advanced. Maybe, you think, you can use this knowledge to help engage him in other activities. But you feel outpaced by him, even though he is only 4 years old. You don't know much about spatial skills, and have always felt you had a poor sense of direction. Sometimes you even mix up right and left! Maybe having Jack in your classroom is giving you an opportunity to learn new skills so you are more comfortable in this area. Are you up to the challenge?

Bravo to the teacher who notices that a student has a strength in spatial skills. Not only are spatial skills difficult to assess, I wonder whether concepts having to do with space are inherently challenging to describe verbally.

Verbal and spatial abilities are so distinct that they are processed in different areas of the brain (Smith, Jonides, & Koeppe, 1996). Experts still do not agree on spatial skill components, though like EF and motor skills, there is consensus that the phrase *spatial skills* is an umbrella term that includes several cognitive processes (Uttal et al., 2013).

In this chapter, I define *spatial skills* and associated terms such as *visuo-motor integration*, review important aspects of spatial development from infancy through the school years, and describe common assessments used in research and clinical practice in early childhood. I also review research efforts to improve spatial skills among children.

> **THEME:** Spatial skills are an underappreciated aspect of learning and school performance. Because of the way that the cognitive processes involved in spatial skills develop, early childhood is an excellent time for teachers to notice and assess children's spatial skills and encourage spatial language.

SPATIAL SKILLS: THINKING ABOUT OBJECTS

With several colleagues, David Uttal, a professor of psychology at Northwestern University and affiliate of the cross-institutional Spatial Intelligence and Learning Center, conducted a meta-analysis of 206 research studies. Their findings led to the team creating a theory of two dimensions of spatial skills (Uttal et al., 2013). These dimensions resulted in five skills that are described in Table 5.1 using the Animal Matching game to illustrate.

The first dimension—*object properties*—has to do with whether spatial information is about a single object (within-object or intrinsic) or about relationships between multiple objects (between-object or extrinsic). The second dimension—*object movement*—has to do with whether the object stays in place (fixed or static) or moves (changing or dynamic).

The top left cell in Table 5.1, under heading Dimension 1, concerns single object properties that do not change. Children draw on this type of spatial skill to recognize objects based on their features. Static within-object skills also allow children to recognize hidden or embedded objects, such as in pictures in magazines or games like "Where's Waldo?" This skill is also referred to as *disembedding* (Mix & Cheng, 2012).

The top right cell in Table 5.1 illustrates between-object properties when the objects don't move or change. This skill pertains to the main goal of the Animal Matching game: remembering where a given card is located in the grid as laid out at the beginning of game play. The object—in this example, the card—does not move within the grid (fixed), and children must remember its location in relation to the other cards on the grid (between-object).

The bottom cells in Table 5.1 are situated in the second overall dimension of object movement, because objects can move or change properties.

The first description in the bottom left cell illustrates the subtype of *transformational* skills when Jack views a card that is upside-down. In this example, an individual card is viewed on its own (within-object) but identifying it requires a transformation through imagining a *rotation* (changing). The second description in the bottom left cell illustrates how Jack uses *spatial visualization* to mentally deconstruct and reconstruct an object based on seeing its pieces or parts.

Even though transformation-rotation and spatial visualization skills are both within-object and dynamic, research suggests that they are not the same skill. Transformations and rotations are especially important for learning geometry, because "geometry requires reasoning about form, angle, and other spatial relations, and thus, may have the most natural affinity to spatial ability of any mathematical ability" (Mix & Cheng, 2012, p. 207).

Finally, the bottom right cell in Table 5.1 shows how a "dynamic mental manipulation" (Uttal et al., 2013, p. 354) is needed when the spatial information about multiple objects is both extrinsic and changing. Jack must remember the location of one or two cards in relation to the entire matrix, but because he is so good at the game, Jack himself moves, so he views the entire matrix from a different perspective. A similar effect would occur if Jack stays in one spot, but the game is placed on a rotating platform like a lazy Susan.

Table 5.1. Two-Dimensional Definition of Spatial Skills Mapped onto the Animal Matching Game

DIMENSION 1: OBJECT PROPERTIES		
	Within-object (intrinsic)	Between-object (extrinsic)
DIMENSION 2: OBJECT MOVEMENT — Fixed (static)	Jack recognizes the mother giraffe based on the animal's features. Jack distinguishes the giraffe from other animals with long necks, such as an ostrich (example of disembedding).	Jack remembers that the mother giraffe is shown on the middle card in the top row of a 3 x 3 matrix (example of spatial perception).
DIMENSION 2: OBJECT MOVEMENT — Changing (dynamic)	Jack recognizes the mother giraffe even when the card is upside down (example of transformation-rotation subtype). Jack identifies a giraffe if he sees separate pictures of different giraffe body parts: long neck, head with large eyes and upright ears, spotted body, skinny legs (example of spatial visualization subtype).	Even after the teacher changes Jack's game play position by rotating him 90 degrees clockwise, Jack can remember that the mother giraffe card is the middle card in the leftmost column of the same 3 x 3 matrix (example of egocentric transformation).

COGNITIVE PROCESSES INVOLVED IN SPATIAL SKILLS

One reason spatial skills are difficult to define is that many spatial tasks do not clearly map onto a certain dimension or single cognitive process. Instead, most spatial tasks vary along these two dimensions of intrinsic or extrinsic, and each involves multiple overlapping processes.

Even so, several specific cognitive processes contribute to spatial skills during the early childhood period and are important for teachers to understand. These processes include perceptual skills, spatial working memory, transformational skills, and constructional skills.

Perceptual Skills

In Chapter 4, I mentioned how perception plays a role in motor skills. With regard to spatial skills, perception means noticing distinctive or important aspects of visual input—or in the case of a child who is visually impaired, tactile or auditory information—that tell about the spatial properties of something.

Perceptual skills are the first step in identifying members of a category, such as animals with floppy ears; distinguishing elements of letters or numerals; or assessing whether a puzzle piece is a middle or edge piece. If children don't notice that a rabbit's ears are big and floppy but a squirrel's ears are tiny, they may have trouble learning to tell the difference between the two animals.

As another example, if children don't see that the letters *b* and *d* are made up of a half-circle and a line, they will have trouble learning those letters and realizing that the line is on the left side of the half-circle in the *b* and the right side in the *d*.

Finally, using a puzzle example, children must first notice—whether from looking or touching or both—the straight side of the edge piece to complete a puzzle. Spatial perceptual skills are also used in matching games or any situation involving comparisons between an object and a target (Miyake et al., 2001)—for example, in an art activity where children paint what they see.

Spatial Working Memory

The next steps after perception include assigning meaning to the information that is perceived, and keeping it in mind long enough to remember and match it with additional information and make a decision, if necessary.

Recall from Chapter 3 that working memory means that information is both *stored* (e.g., "Remember these two lists of five digits") and *processed* or manipulated (e.g., "Remember the biggest number from both lists and reorder them in order from smallest to largest"). Spatial working memory entails storing *spatial* information and manipulating it as new information comes in.

Many tasks require children to compare information they already have in their minds with new information. For example, in the Animal Matching game, Jack needs to store and retrieve information about the cards he has already turned over so he can compare the animals he has seen to new cards that his peers turn over.

Transformational Skills

Spatial working memory plays a central role whenever children must perform what are called *transformations*. This term implies that an object is being transformed, or *changed*, in some way. Sometimes the change happens only in spatial working memory, but other times, children use their spatial working memory to imagine a transformation that they then carry out in real life (see next section on constructional skills).

In adults, there are two types of transformations: changes to the spatial properties or location of an object—called *object transformations*—and changes to the spatial properties or location of oneself—called *egocentric transformations* (Zacks, Mires, Tversky, & Hazeltine, 2001). The teacher asking Jack to rotate his spot around the Animal Matching game is an example of an egocentric transformation, which I discuss later in this chapter. Studies conducted with children support the same two categories of transformation emerging by the end of early childhood (Crescentini, Fabbro, & Urgesi, 2014).

As you can see in the previous examples, a common type of object-based transformation is a *rotation*, such as when Jack identifies a mother giraffe card, even though the card is rotated so that the animal he sees is upside-down. In this example, the rotation occurs in the horizontal dimension, like the ticking of analog clock hands that rotate around the clock face. Rotations can also occur in 3D, such as when Jack turns cards from face-up to facedown. Other types of transformations include a revolution of an object around a space, change in size, or change in properties such as Jack imagining cutting an animal card in half.

To transform objects in their minds, children must form accurate mental representations of the object, which goes back to the importance of perception. The term *representation* refers to how children imagine the object appearing, before and after any mental changes to the object.

Constructional Skills: The Special Case of Visuo-Motor Integration

Constructional skills mean that children are able to construct or make something that didn't exist before, either in their imaginations or using tangible materials. Both drawing and copying an image are examples of 2D constructional skills, which also rely on perceptual skills and accurate mental representations of the object to be created or copied. Building or copying an existing model made out of objects or manipulatives are examples of 3D constructional skills.

For early childhood professionals, the word *copying* may have negative connotations, calling to mind rote instruction, thoughtless reproduction, and no room for creativity. Isn't it better to create something new from an idea generated in one's mind than to copy someone else's work?

There are certainly many contexts, from writing assignments throughout school to art class, where originality wins. Yet, when it comes to copying, there is more going on, neurologically, than meets the eye, so to speak. Some of the most interesting research in this area has been conducted in Japan with adults—both typically developing and those with Williams syndrome. Poor spatial skills are one of the main characteristics of individuals with Williams syndrome (Kim & Cameron, 2016), and attempts to understand the way they process spatial information has revealed insights that are relevant for the general population.

From what is available in English translations, it's clear that copying is very important to the development of spatial skills. When copying an image, individuals exhibit more activity in a greater number of brain areas than when tracing (Ogawa, Erato, & Inui, 2010). Unlike tracing and drawing, copying requires children to perform transformations and make comparisons between the model and the copy, to use spatial working memory to hold the model in mind while looking at their version, and to monitor their progress and correct errors. Thus, multiple processes described earlier in this chapter are required to copy successfully.

As such, copying is a *visuo-motor integration* task, where children integrate their visual perceptions with their movements (Beery, Buktenica, & Beery, 2010). The integration of visual information with motor behaviors is another reason that copying is a special process, with exciting implications for the school-readiness period. I return to constructional skills and tasks that support them in Chapter 9.

DEVELOPMENT OF SPATIAL SKILLS IN INFANCY AND CHILDHOOD

Esther Thelen (1941–2004) was a famous scholar of infant and child development who studied babies acquiring motor milestones such as how to crawl or walk. Her research led her to conclude that the process of learning and achieving cognitive milestones can't be separated from our perceptions, emotions, and movements. This is because the brain is housed within our bodies, and our bodies help us navigate through the world.

Together with our perceptions, which change whenever we move, our emotions provide us with signals about the safety, comfort, and possibilities of our surroundings. Therefore, most of the learning that children do depends on these so-called *embodied* experiences. The power of embodiment applies to a surprising range of skills, including some types of vocabulary development, as discussed in Chapter 7, but especially to spatial skills.

Perceptual Skills Develop Early and Through Experience

One fascinating study with infants illustrates the power of experience in how we develop perceptual spatial skills. As a graduate student at New York University (NYU), Kasey Soska wondered whether infants' sitting experience might be related to their understanding of how objects looked from different angles. The reasoning behind this hypothesis is that as soon as infants can sit up, a new world opens to objects that can be more readily picked up, held, mouthed, turned around, and passed from hand to hand. Walking is an even bigger milestone that brings more possibilities for learning (Campos et al., 2000).

The NYU research team studied 28 infants between ages 4.5 and 7.5 months who had a variety of independent sitting experiences. They observed the babies playing with toys in the lab, and also asked parents about how well and by when their child could sit.

Results showed that babies who had relatively more sitting experience, and babies who used their eyes and hands together to play with objects, better understood 3D objects presented on a 2D screen than babies with less sitting experience, or who didn't use their eyes and hands to play (Soska, Adolph, & Johnson, 2010). This means that infants' insight about objects as 3D depended on both their sitting experience and their hand-eye coordination.

In Figure 5.1, what do you see? Do you see a 3D box, rather than a square with two small triangles and two small trapezoids? Your perception of a 2D stimuli as a 3D object is similar to how infants' understanding of space was assessed in the NYU study.

Figure 5.1. 2D Visual Representation That Most People Perceive as 3D

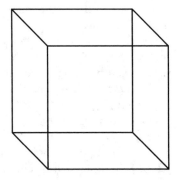

That some infants can already perceive a set of uniquely arranged lines on a screen as representing an object in three dimensions alludes to the importance of perceptual skills emerging early in development. Consistent with this view, in a study of 80 Italian children between ages 3 and 5, those in the youngest group (3- to 3.5-year-olds) could already perform at the highest level on a task that required perceptual skills (Del Giudice et al., 2000).

Specifically, in this study, children were shown a group of 20 dots, and then the examiner pretended to draw imaginary lines through some of the dots. The children's job was to count the number of dots that were intersected by each imaginary line. The 20 children in the 3-year-old group scored on average 19.1 out of 20, whereas the 20 children in the next older group, 3.5- to 4-year-olds, scored on average 20 out of 20. It is rare to find perfect scores when assessing such young children.

Development of Spatial Working Memory

Spatial working memory draws on representational skills where children imagine an image in their minds. In contrast with perceptual skills, the Italian research group found that representational skills had started to develop among 4-year-olds, but the children were still not expert by age 9. This is consistent with research on the development of spatial working memory, which is an advanced skill set that is part of EF (see also Chapter 3).

Developmentally, by age 6 in a sample of 736 children from different backgrounds in England, short-term memory for words was a separate skill from short-term memory for spatial features (Gathercole, Pickering, Ambridge, & Wearing, 2004). (Remember from Chapter 3 that short-term memory refers to storage only, and is a separate skill from true working memory that involves both storage and processing.) Children younger than age 6 have very limited working memory, and researchers have developed other types of measures that do not make the heavy cognitive demands of traditional working memory tasks developed for adults (Roman, Pisoni, & Kronenberger, 2014).

What does this mean for early childhood professionals? Working memory is in short supply in young children, and so it is not reasonable to expect children to remember locations of items when carrying out multistep directions, or to keep track of very much extra information while they are learning something new. For example, even if you have reminded children several times that a visitor is coming to read a book at the end of free-choice time today, they may forget to incorporate this information into their play plans, and plan a longer activity than is reasonable.

Influences on working memory arise from both genes and environment, including the experience of attending preschool and kindergarten (Burrage et al., 2008; Stins et al., 2005). In other words, children's working memory improves over time, and learning experiences matter in early childhood as well as in infancy. The contributions of both age and experience are also clear when examining how transformational and constructional skills develop.

Development of Transformational and Constructional Skills

Spatial working memory underlies transformational and constructional skills. Partially because they heavily rely on working memory, transformational and constructional skills develop later than perceptual skills (Del Giudice et al., 2000).

The role of age in transformational skill emergence. Recall that object-based transformations mean that children can imagine changes to an external object, such as what a dollhouse looks like from the other side. In contrast, egocentric transformations mean that children are able to imagine changes to their own body orientation, such as identifying which hand of a manikin they are facing is marked gray. To correctly respond on such a task means participants imagine turning themselves to face the same direction as the manikin. Research with children ages 7 to 11 years shows that object-based transformations develop by 7 years of age, whereas egocentric transformations develop later, around age 8 (Crescentini et al., 2014).

You may find it interesting to know that 8-year-olds whose teachers rated them lower in cooperativeness and empathy had more difficulty imagining egocentric transformations. The researchers think that age 8 is when children are developing the ability to imagine their own bodies moving around a reference point. Children's focus on themselves and their shifting perspectives may make it more difficult to take the perspectives of other people—both metaphorically (seeing another's viewpoint) and literally (seeing from another's physical perspective).

Spatial language and children's spatial skills. Some fascinating research regarding young children's spatial skill development concerns how caregivers talk to and play with their children. To look at caregiver talk, developmental psychologists from Florida International University and the University of Chicago used a special coding system to label the type and amount of spatial language that parents used in structured play situations with their preschool-age children (Pruden, Levine, & Huttenlocher, 2011). The sample included 52 typically developing children ages 14–46 months. Most parents had a college degree and made at least $50,000 per year, but families from low-SES backgrounds also participated in the study.

Examples of spatial language were words about dimension and size, such as *large, small,* or *skinny*; words about shapes, such as *triangle* or *square*; and words about spatial properties, such as *edge, pointy,* or *curvy*.

Other spatial words were about location and relative position, such as *above*, *below*, *next to*, or *beneath*, but these words were not studied because they overlapped too much with general language use.

The research team observed the child and a parent in everyday interactions in their homes. Across nine visits lasting about 90 minutes each, the average number of spatial words parents used altogether was 167, but the minimum number was only 5, and the maximum was 525. Even though 167 spatial words represents less than 0.1% of the total words spoken by parents in the visits, the research team found that children whose parents used relatively more spatial words at home performed better on two out of three spatial skills assessments than children whose parents spoke fewer spatial words.

The first assessment asked children to imagine a transformation on a pictured object. The second assessment presented a picture, such as a dog to the right of a house, and showed children four boxes with a dot placed either above, below, to the left, or to the right (the correct answer) of the box. The second assessment is called "Spatial Analogies" and tests if children understand whether abstract symbols can represent real-life spatial relations. In adults, this skill would be similar to map reading.

There are two important nuances to these findings: First, parents' spatial language was related to children's spatial skills through *children's* spatial language. In other words, parents who used relatively more spatial words had children who used relatively more spatial words, and it was those children whose speech was rich in spatial words who scored the best of all children in the study on the two tests of spatial skills. This pattern illustrates how important it is for caregivers to interact with children and invite them to actively engage and talk about spatial features, properties, and relationships during play situations.

Second, research at the University of Wisconsin shows that it is not just the quantity of spatial words that children use, but the quality of their talk about spatial relationships (Miller, Vlach, & Simmering, 2016). Researchers asked 41 4-year-olds (mostly White, mid-SES) to tell a stuffed animal named Bucky the location of an object in a picture displayed on PowerPoint slides. Bucky was not looking at the screen, and children were discouraged from using their hands to indicate the object's location.

Children who described the context of an object (for example, "The book is on the table") had better spatial skills than children who only referred to the book's existence ("There is the book"). This pattern emerged even after accounting for the total number of spatial and general vocabulary words that children knew.

This finding reminds us that spatial skills are essentially about noticing and understanding objects (or oneself) in relation to a certain context. Even though verbal processes are generally separate from spatial ones, children's language about spatial concepts is also a window to their spatial skills. Later, in Chapters 9 and 10, I describe guided object play, which creates the context for teachers to have conversations with children about spatial features and concepts.

> **EXERCISE:** On a piece of lined paper, make three columns, and label them "Dimension/Size," "Shapes," and "Spatial Properties" (the spatial language categories that Pruden et al. (2011) used in their spatial language study. Time yourself for 3 minutes, and write down as many words as you can in each column.

ASSESSING SPATIAL SKILLS IN EARLY CHILDHOOD

There are two main types of spatial skills assessments for young children: subtests embedded in larger published test batteries and tests developed by researchers specifically to measure a particular aspect of spatial skill.

Both types of assessments can be prohibitive for early childhood professionals, either because of cost, in the case of published test batteries, or because of the specialized materials and credentials needed to administer the assessment. Thus, the concerns about access that I discussed in Chapters 3 and 4 for EF and motor skills also apply to measuring spatial skills.

Although scholars are trying to bring more attention to spatial skills in early childhood, they are not prominent parts of early childhood education, partly because of their neglect in early childhood teacher preparation (Berkowicz & Myers, 2017; Clements & Sarama, 2011). A Johns Hopkins University nonprofit called the Center for Talented Youth points out that many students who are gifted in spatial skills are not identified by the verbal- and number-focused testing so common in schools (Stumpf, Mills, Brody, & Baxley, 2013). Public awareness of the role of spatial skills for later achievement in science, technology, engineering, and mathematics (STEM) is growing (Wai, Lubinski, & Benbow, 2009), however. Preparing students for participating in today's globalized world makes it all the more crucial to accurately assess and promote children's spatial skills.

Table 5.2 displays several spatial skills assessments, including details for obtaining the assessment, the age range for the assessment, and the cognitive process measured with a brief task description. This is not an exhaustive list, but is meant to introduce you to some of the ways that spatial skills are assessed in young children. Notice how the first three tasks require mainly mental work, whereas the two latter, constructional tasks require children to do mental work and also produce a copy of a model.

Table 5.2. Examples of Spatial Skills Assessments

Assessment, Publisher, Cost	Author	Age Range	Cognitive Process and Task Description
Arrows subtest of the revised Developmental NEuroPSYchological Assessment (NEPSY-II), Pearson, complete kit costs $950; PhD or clinical credentials required	(Korkman, Kirk, & Kemp, 2007)	3:0 to 16:0	Perceptual skills; children view a target dot, then choose the one of several arrows that is pointing directly at the dot
Missing Scan Test (MST), On request from the authors	(Roman, Pisoni, & Kronenberger, 2014)	3:0 to 5:0	Spatial working memory; children watch animals go into a barn, then must remember "which one is missing" when all but one come back out
Children's Mental Transformation Task (CMTT); contact the author	(Levine, Huttenlocher, Taylor, & Langrock, 1999)	4:0 to 6:11	Transformational skills; children view two target shapes, then decide which of four composite shapes the two target shapes could make
Visuo-motor integration subtest of the Beery VMI, Pearson, $149 for complete test kit	(Beery, Buktenica, & Beery, 2010)	2:0 to 99:11	Constructional skills; children copy a series of increasingly challenging designs with a pencil
Test of Spatial Assembly (TOSA); contact the authors	(Verdine, Golinkoff, Hirsh-Pasek, & Newcombe, 2017)	3:0 to 5:0	Constructional skills in 2D and 3D; children copy a target arrangement using geometric shapes (2D trials) or interlocking blocks (3D trials)

REVIEW OF RESEARCH TO IMPROVE SPATIAL SKILLS

As introduced earlier, researchers surveyed 206 different research studies since 1984 that tried to improve participants' spatial skills (Uttal et al., 2013). They concluded that spatial skills can be trained; in other words, people who receive training in spatial skills will improve on those skills. In research terms, this is a strong claim and is warranted because the researchers included only studies that had an experimental design. This means that study participants were randomly assigned to receive the spatial skills training or a control experience. Both the training and control groups were the same before the training was delivered, so any differences following their participation can be assumed to arise from the training itself (see Chapter 6 for more information about types of research studies).

Of the 206 studies in the Uttal et al. (2013) review, 26%, or 53 of them, were conducted with children under age 13. To understand this issue better, I looked at the studies in the review that were conducted in the early childhood period (ages 3 to 8) and that were published in 2000 or later. Unfortunately, only three studies (Studies 1–3 in the next two paragraphs) fell into this category, plus an additional study that was designed with 2nd- to 4th-graders in mind but tested only 4th-graders. I decided to include the last study with 4th-graders to illustrate the range of methods that improve children's spatial skills (Study 4).

Interestingly, even with such a small number, the four studies varied considerably in methods and participants: Study 1, with 47 3rd-graders (8- to 9-year-olds) from New Jersey, used the game Tetris™ to improve children's mental rotation skills (De Lisi & Wolford, 2002). Study 2, with 600 children (5-, 6-, 7-, 8-, and 9-year-olds) from Missouri, used water bottles tipped at different angles to teach children that the water level will stay horizontal with the floor, regardless of the angle of the tip (Parameswaran, 2003).

Study 3, with 80 5-year-olds from the Chicago area, had children practice with special wood cutouts to learn to identify the whole shape that could be made with separate cutout parts (Ehrlich, Levine, & Goldin-Meadow, 2006); this is similar to the Test of Spatial Assembly (TOSA) shown in Table 5.2. Finally, Study 4 used a diverse map-skills curriculum designed for 2nd- to 4th-graders to improve the map skills of two dozen 9- and 10-year-olds (4th-graders only). The curriculum included computers, hands-on activities in the classroom, and active lessons outside on the space represented on the map.

Based on their statistics, Uttal et al. (2013) concluded that spatial skills training can work for children as well as adults. Still, the success of each intervention varied considerably, especially for the studies that included younger children. What's more, an intervention that helped participants get better at one spatial skill, such as mental rotation, didn't necessarily mean that participants improved on other spatial skills. Much remains to be learned about what types of experiences are most important for young children to expand their spatial skills.

Because of the close coupling between spatial skills and mathematics, I return to this issue in Chapter 8 when I describe interventions that have improved both spatial and mathematics skills in young children. Finally, in Chapter 9, I share results from an after-school intervention that used constructional tasks to improve children's spatial skills and executive function. In Chapter 10, I propose guided object play as an activity to promote spatial skills.

SUMMARY

Spatial skills are complex to put into words, but have to do with understanding the properties and movements of objects or individuals, including ourselves. Spatial skills rely on perceptual skills, spatial working memory, transformational skills, and constructional skills, which develop at different rates. Assessing and supporting spatial skills is important beginning in early childhood because achievement in science, technology, engineering, arts, and mathematics (STEAM) domains relies on spatial competence. Based on evidence that spatial skills can be improved with a variety of interventions, teachers can use spatial vocabulary words and activities to help young children notice, describe, and transform objects and their environments.

Learning Spatial Skills with Jack and the Other Children

After learning about the different types of spatial skills, you decide to encourage Jack's passion for spatial games. You teach the children words like *middle*, *top*, and *bottom* and have them pay attention to the features and placement of the cards in the Animal Matching game.

When Jack makes a match, you describe his actions with words—for example, "Jack chose the middle card. When he turns it over, he sees the giraffe's brown ears on the white background, and he can tell the card is upside-down." The children think that you talking this way sounds funny at first, but they become used to it. You notice that when they're not playing the game, some children use spatial words you hadn't heard them say before.

Part III

LINKING THE LEARNING DOMAINS AND THE FOUNDATIONAL COGNITIVE SKILLS

CHAPTER 6

Connections Between the Foundational Cognitive Skills and Nonacademic Skills

Physical Development, Social-Emotional Development, and Approaches to Learning

Alicia, whom we met in Chapter 4, loves any activity that involves a ball, but she isn't allowed to play outside in her neighborhood. There are too many cars near her house, and the neighborhood basketball court usually has much older children who look like adults to Alicia. Her mother asks her to play indoors most of the time, but the apartment is so small that there aren't many options other than TV and playing computer games on her mom's cell phone. So, Alicia spends a lot of the time siting on the couch. During outside time, when the other children chase one another, Alicia sits on the sidelines. She knows she is clumsy, and her peers know it, too. Things just seem easier if she watches instead of trying to join.

In the classroom, you know Alicia to be quiet and reasonable. She always follows your requests, but sometimes when you review her work, you see that she doesn't grasp some important concepts. You once heard Alicia whisper, "I can't do this," when you asked the children to line themselves up by height. When you encouraged her in the direction of her spot, she accidentally bumped into a child, who scowled and said, "I don't want to stand by Clumsy Alicia." You worry about Alicia's self-concept, and whether she will be able to make friends in kindergarten.

Alicia's story shows how interconnected motor skills are with other areas of development, especially social-emotional development. In this chapter, I examine links among the foundational cognitive skills, and social-emotional learning (SEL), physical development, and approaches to learning, which are considered nonacademic domains in the Head Start framework.

> **THEME:** Connections among foundational cognitive skills and nonacademic areas can be found throughout the school years, but are especially pronounced in early childhood. Whether children

can develop healthy social relationships and adaptive classroom behavior depends on good physical health, including adequate motor skills and strong self-control. Spatial skills—specifically, visuo-motor integration—relate to how well children approach learning tasks in the classroom.

In Chapter 1, I briefly reviewed how the U.S. Department of Education convened a group of experts who defined five distinct school readiness domains (National Education Goals Panel, 1995). As a reminder, these overarching readiness domains include: (1) perceptual, motor, and physical development; (2) social and emotional development; (3) approaches toward learning; (4) language and literacy; and (5) cognition.

In their study of how these domains were reflected in U.S. learning standards across 46 states, Scott-Little et al. (2006) noticed that the five domains fit under two even broader categories: on one hand, the *academic* domains of language and cognition; and on the other, *nonacademic* domains of physical and motor development, social and emotional development, and approaches toward learning.

Even though state standards tend to emphasize academic domains, a broad base of research supports the importance of the nonacademic learning domains for children's overall well-being and development. The three foundational cognitive skills—EF, motor skills, and spatial skills—also connect with the three nonacademic domains to support school readiness.

HOW FITNESS AND NUTRITION MATTER FOR EF

Though we may think about children's physical health and development as having to do with their bodies, health and nutrition also affect the developing brain and how well information is processed. Unfortunately, many early childhood educators do not think of their classroom as the right place to encourage children to learn about and adopt healthy eating and exercise habits (Lu & Montague, 2016). Instead, educators view these topics as matters for families to decide.

Indeed, people have strong feelings about food, and concerns about weight and health can be difficult topics for even medical doctors to broach with their patients. But during early childhood, bringing physical development into preschool and early elementary settings may help teachers better prepare children for learning and school, because of the intriguing connections between children's physical and cognitive selves.

One area of research examines how delay of gratification, the type of inhibitory control involved in waiting for a reward, is related to children's choices about food. Some children succeed in delaying gratification when their environment offers engaging activities that serve as alternatives to eating. For example, one study of 241 overweight 9-year-olds found that children who chose money over food in a computer-based task lost more weight over 16 weeks of an intervention, but only if they also had access to healthy foods and interesting activities or exercise equipment at home (Best et al., 2012).

Consistent with the idea that children must have attractive alternatives to eating and sedentary activities, the American Academy of Pediatrics (AAP) recommends emphasizing healthy *behaviors*, not weight and appearance, for youth (Golden, Schneider, & Wood, 2016). The AAP have recommended for some time that physical activity be part of young children's daily lives (AAP Council on Early Childhood and AAP Council on School Health, 2016; Burdette & Whitaker, 2005).

In a review of interventions to improve executive function for children ages 4 to 12, programs like tai chi and aerobics that incorporate movement tend to have the longest-lasting effects (Diamond & Lee, 2011). But movement alone is not enough, because in studies of exercise programs, only programs where children exercise vigorously—that is, sweat and breathe hard—for at least 20 minutes appear to benefit cognitive skills (C. L. Davis et al., 2011). This may be because of the "positive challenge or stress to the brain" during strenuous exercise, which includes benefits to hormones, stress responses, and changes in the parts of the brain where EF occurs (Sattelmair & Ratey, 2009, p. 366).

Laura Chaddock-Heyman and Charles Hillman of the University of Illinois-Champaign Urbana and their colleagues (2014) conducted a series of studies to understand how children's fitness is reflected in their brains and in how well they can learn.

First, they report that children who are more physically fit process certain types of information more efficiently than children who are overweight. More specifically, in laboratory tasks to assess memory requiring EF, physically fit children have an easier time focusing their attention where needed and inhibiting impulsive responding. These advantages appear to translate into a more realistic setting such as a simulation of trying to cross the street while distracted (Chaddock-Heyman, Hillman, Cohen, & Kramer, 2014). Children who are more physically active also have larger structures in the brain, including the basal ganglia and hippocampus, which are associated with controlling attention and making memories, respectively (Chaddock et al., 2010).

This research alludes to the importance of physical health and development for EF, as well as the role of environment. The research in this area has some limitations, however. First, researchers have mostly studied middle childhood and adolescence, rather than including children under age 8. In addition, most research that includes children is *cross-sectional*, not longitudinal or experimental. The term *cross-sectional* means that researchers compare children who are physically fit with those who aren't. In contrast, *longitudinal* research follows the same children over time, and in *experimental* research, different groups are randomly given different fitness experiences.

The type of study that lends the strongest support to the idea that interventions in one area—say, improving physical fitness—affect a particular skill like EF, is experimental. In experimental studies, it is appropriate to say that the intervention *caused* change in the desired outcome.

As I noted in Chapter 5, in experiments, children are randomly assigned to either the intervention group or a control group. Random assignment is important because then the only explanation for any differences between the two groups at the end of the study is that one group received the intervention and the other group did not.

Among elementary and adolescent children, a growing number of experimental studies using random assignment suggests that certain types of physical activity can cause changes in the brain with benefits to memory processes related to EF, specifically. For example, Monti, Hillman, and Cohen (2012) randomly assigned 25 9-year-olds to an aerobic exercise after-school program (intervention), and 19 9-year-olds to do whatever they normally did after school. The students in the aerobic after-school program did 2 hours of physical activity every day after school for 9 months.

At the end of the intervention, those in the aerobic program were actually more physically fit, as measured by a test of how much oxygen they used during a treadmill exercise. What's more, children in the aerobic program were also faster at recognizing paired images compared to children in the control group. This type of memory is associated with the hippocampus of the brain, which "talks to" the EF area (prefrontal cortex) in memory tasks where two or more images have been paired together.

This study is exciting because it shows that exercise changes the brain for the better. Still, it doesn't tell us if exercise can benefit children in the real world of the classroom. Addressing this issue, Goh (2017) trained teachers of 3rd-, 4th-, and 5th-graders to intersperse their academic lessons with active lessons. Results showed that students were more active at the end of 10 weeks of active lessons than at the beginning, and that students' on-task behavior, which relies on EF, increased over time.

These studies are promising, but we need to know more about appropriate activity levels associated with benefits to the brain and EF processes in the early childhood period (Chaddock-Heyman et al., 2014). Results for younger age groups show patterns that are similar to those with relatively older children: For example, Becker, McClelland, Loprinzi, and Trost (2014) found that among 51 preschoolers who exhibited varying amounts of active play during recess, those who engaged in more active play had better behavioral self-regulation (closely related to EF; see also Chapter 3).

Because Alicia from the vignette opening this chapter often sits out of activities, she is therefore deprived of the benefits of exercising both her body and her EF. In the next section, I explore how motor skills intersect with the second nonacademic school-readiness domain, social-emotional development.

> *EXERCISE:* When young children are asked to coordinate their bodies to balance and move through space, such as in the spoon-carrying exercise in traditional Montessori classroom, they must also focus their attention on the task and ignore distractions (Lillard, 2005). This type of task, with a goal and ongoing challenge, therefore offers children the opportunity to practice EF along with their motor skills. Can you think of another exercise that allows children to practice EF while they move?

THE ROLE OF MOTOR SKILLS IN CHILDREN'S SELF-CONFIDENCE

Social-emotional development, also known as social-emotional learning, is another so-called "nonacademic" domain of school readiness. In other fields such as economics, SEL is called a "noncognitive" skill (Potter et al., 2012). This unfortunate phrasing, which undercuts the importance of noncognitive skills, simply signifies any skills that achievement and IQ tests do not assess directly.

Another flaw in the term *nonacademic* is the implication that these skills are not relevant for learning. Yet teachers and others who work with children know that being ready for school means much more than knowing particular facts, recognizing patterns, or processing information quickly. For example, if a child is distracted, angry, or otherwise preoccupied, learning and applying their cognitive skills to a situation is difficult, if not impossible.

Not surprisingly, teachers of young children endorse many skills that are part of social-emotional development, such as working in groups or independently, as incredibly important for a smooth transition to school (Rimm-Kaufman et al., 2000). Teachers report that many kindergartners struggle to establish adaptive social-emotional skills at school entry, which sets children up for a difficult time throughout the year (Ladd, Birch, & Buhs, 1999).

Social-emotional skills include those skills needed to understand one's own and others' feelings, desires, and social signals. The Collaborative for Academic, Social, and Emotional Learning (CASEL), which is based in Chicago, defines five specific skills that comprise SEL (Greenberg et al., 2003). The first two—self-management and self-awareness—have to do with whether a child notices and can control their own emotions and responses. The other three skills—social awareness, relationship skills, and responsible decisionmaking—have to do with whether children notice and act appropriately in response to others' emotions given the context.

Similar to assessments for EF, valid and accessible early childhood assessments of skills in the area of social-emotional development are difficult to find (Denham, 2006). Still, even though it is used in SEL, EF is not the same as SEL. My colleagues and I have argued that SEL is one of the more complex arenas in which children need to exercise the cognitive processes of EF (McClelland, Cameron, Wanless, et al., 2007).

For example, in the simple lining-up activity described in the vignette at the beginning of this chapter, Alicia must listen to her teacher's instructions to line up by height, remember that "height" means how tall she is, notice where her peers are standing, decide where she might fit, and then navigate into the spot—potentially while ignoring or responding appropriately to the rude comment from her peer. In terms of SEL, a child who has trouble performing motor tasks may exhibit frustration, have more conflict with peers, or simply avoid particular activities or situations.

In two studies I was a part of, we asked teachers from Virginia and South Carolina to rate their 386 kindergarten, 1st-, and 2nd-grade students using the Motor Skills Rating Scale (MSRS) described in Chapter 4. We found that children whose teachers rated them as being good at the motor skills needed in the classroom—such as tying their shoes, managing learning materials, and manipulating writing utensils—performed better on a wide range of measures, including measures of social-emotional learning (Cameron, Chen, et al., 2012; Kim et al., 2015).

And what about those children who have trouble with motor skills? As you might expect, students who struggle with movement difficulties also find school challenging (Pagani & Messier, 2012; Visser, 2003), including the 5–10% of children diagnosed with developmental coordination disorder, or DCD (see also Chapter 4).

Before its introduction into the *Diagnostic and Statistical Manual* in 1989, DCD used to be referred as "clumsy child syndrome," and children who are clumsy suffer cascading social-emotional consequences: Like Alicia, they often lack the confidence to participate in sports or games, which is likely to worsen if peers reject them socially (Skinner & Piek, 2001).

Much of the research that links motor skills with debilitating social-emotional outcomes has been conducted with special populations such as children with disabilities or a developmental delay. The clinical nature of this research obscures its relevance for the early childhood period, before most children receive a specific diagnosis. But scientists are also finding similar patterns among typically developing children.

For example, Australian researchers Wilson, Piek, and Kane (2013) measured motor skills, social skills, and internalizing symptoms such as social withdrawal and depression among 475 4- to 6-year-olds. They used a 14-item individual assessment of motor skills and teacher reports of children's social skills on the one hand and signs of depression such as low mood, nervousness, anxiety, and physical complaints like a stomachache on the other. Their study used a statistical analysis called *mediation*, and also measured children's age, gender, and IQ.

Including age, gender, and IQ in the analysis gives more confidence that study results are due to specific connections among motor, social, and emotional domains, rather than because of something else, such as children with low IQ having lower scores on all three measures of interest or older children having better scores on all measures. And even though a mediation analysis doesn't allow researchers to conclude that poor motor skills *cause* other negative outcomes, the analysis tests hypotheses about the possible contribution of poor motor skills to other aspects of development and informs interventions.

The first important result in Wilson et al.'s study (2013) was that children with poor motor skills were more likely to be rated by their teachers as having poor social skills. In turn, children with worse social skills were more likely to turn their negative emotions inward and to suffer more symptoms such as stomachaches.

The explanation that the researchers offered is that children with poor motor skills remove themselves but are also are excluded by peers from activities where they might have the opportunity to learn social skills. In other words, studies show that children with poor motor skills behave like Alicia, who both took herself out of play situations and was shut out by her peers. This negative cycle only continues as Alicia spends increasing amounts of time by herself in other school situations.

Sadly, even though teachers may perceive children like Alicia as well behaved, the child herself may not see things that way. Harter and Pike (1984) found that children ages 4 to 6 view their skills in academic, gross motor, and social arenas as all related. Taking such a general view of themselves is positive for those children who have a lot of confidence ("If I'm good at drawing, then I must be good at making friends and playing basketball too!") but unhealthy for those children with a more negative view of themselves.

> *EXERCISE:* Teachers can help children who may have difficulties in a certain area of motor development by providing opportunities to practice and succeed in that area. Teachers can also make a point to notice and point out to the withdrawn or sad child their unique strengths and successes. Think of one or two children in your class who struggle with motor skills. What is an activity in which they succeed, and what specific phrase would you say to encourage this child?

APPROACHES TO LEARNING: CONNECTIONS TO EF AND SPATIAL SKILLS

The third nonacademic domain in the Head Start school-readiness framework is called approaches to learning. While the domain of social-emotional learning emphasizes children developing healthy *social relationships* with caregivers, teachers, and peers, the approaches to learning domain emphasizes whether children engage effectively with classroom *learning opportunities*. To discern a child's approaches to learning, consider questions like these:

- Are children *curious*, excited, and eager to learn, or hesitant?
- Do they show *initiative* by sharing their own ideas within the constraints of the opportunity, or do they just want to be told what to do?
- How do children respond when they get stuck or the task doesn't go the way they expected? Do they become frustrated, or do they show *persistence* and try again?

The italicized words—*curious, initiative,* and *persistence*—are general and abstract, and call to mind other abstract concepts such as attitude, motivation, and creativity. Among young children, however, demonstrating adaptive approaches to learning depends on some extremely concrete skills.

For example, to show curiosity and inventiveness about an activity or a material, children need to be able to pay attention as their teacher explains the opportunity and then understand how the opportunity may be modified or imagined differently. Similarly, to show initiative in deciding to, for example, try a new arts and crafts activity, children must be able to navigate to the area, arrange their bodies appropriately, and use both motor and spatial skills to choose and use materials. Finally, to successfully complete a learning activity takes self-control to persist through challenge and ignore distractions such as leaving to play with friends or visit another tantalizing center.

In other words, all three foundational cognitive skills play a role in children being able to demonstrate effective approaches to learning. In the next section, I emphasize EF and spatial skills.

How EF Contributes to Approaches to Learning

Usually, children's approaches to learning are measured by asking teachers about individual students' behaviors toward and during classroom learning tasks. In one study, using the same type of mediation analysis I described earlier, Vitiello and colleagues (2011) examined how EF and teacher-rated approaches to learning relate to one another and to children's academic readiness. They used *cognitive control theory*, which states that an EF process within a child can be applied to a higher-order, more complex situation of a classroom, and thereby prove important to a child's academic and learning goals (Johnson, Chang, & Lord, 2006).

Participants in Vitiello et al.'s (2011) study were 191 mostly African American children attending Head Start in southern Florida. The researchers' measure of EF assessed the cognitive flexibility component by asking children to pick the "odd picture out" according to criteria that changed. For example, first, children had to choose the picture that pointed the wrong way from other identical pictures; next, they had to choose the picture that was different from the others.

Children's teachers also rated their approaches to learning using the Preschool Learning Behaviors Scale (PLBS; McDermott, Leigh, & Perry, 2002). The PLBS asked if children showed interest in and were motivated to pursue activities (motivation), if they persisted over time (persistence), and if they could tolerate frustrations that arose during activities (attitude). Finally, children's academic school readiness was assessed with the Bracken Basic Concepts Scale–Revised School Readiness Composite (Bracken, 1998).

Looking at the study's results, teachers perceived children with low EF to have lower approaches to learning, because they viewed such children to show less motivation, exhibit worse attitudes, and be less likely to persist through difficult tasks. Children with low EF also scored lower in academic readiness.

There was evidence that these children's lower persistence and motivation contributed to their being less ready for school, academically speaking. Somewhat surprisingly, having a poor attitude—which depended in large part upon the child's classroom membership—was not related to their academic readiness. In other words, only teachers' reports of the child's persistence and motivation—not their attitude—told about their academic readiness.

EF and Spatial Skills Can Compensate for Each Other

Strong foundational cognitive skills are clearly connected to whether children exhibit positive learning behaviors, and there is some evidence that solid levels of one foundational skill could make up for other disadvantages (Liew, Chen, & Hughes, 2010).

In a five-state study of a different group of 467 mostly Latino/a American and African American preschoolers age 3 to 5 years, my colleagues and I analyzed data that included teacher ratings of children's approaches to learning measured with the same Preschool Learning Behaviors Scale (PLBS) as in Vitiello et al.'s (2011) study. For foundational cognitive skills, children's EF was measured with an inhibitory control task requiring them to tap once when the examiner tapped a pencil twice (and tap twice when the examiner tapped once); spatial skills were measured with the Beery VMI test of visuo-motor integration at the beginning of the preschool year (Cameron, Brock, et al., 2015).

We found that two groups of children earned relatively higher ratings from their teachers on approaches to learning in both fall and spring—those who did relatively better on *either* EF or visuo-motor integration, or children who did well on both. The only children who earned significantly lower ratings of approaches to learning from their teachers were those who entered school with weak inhibitory control *and* poor visuo-motor integration.

We explained these findings with a pattern we called *compensatory*: Children with weak inhibitory control were still perceived by their teachers as having adaptive approaches to learning, as long as they had strong visuo-motor integration. Similarly, children with poor visuo-motor integration were perceived by their teachers as having adaptive approaches to learning, as long as they had good inhibitory control. This pattern was strongest for fall ratings of approaches to learning, but also appeared in the same pattern in the spring, controlling for teachers' fall ratings. Having higher-than-average levels of at least one of the two skills was good, but it was slightly better to have good visuo-motor integration than good inhibitory control.

What does this research mean for teachers? Even through 1st grade, children who have good visuo-motor integration are perceived by teachers to function better in the classroom (Kim et al., 2016)—perhaps because so many school activities require fine motor skills and visuo-motor integration (see also Chapter 4). Knowing this, teachers who notice that children have strong inhibitory control can encourage them to persist while working on spatial and motor tasks that are difficult for them, such as during arts and crafts centers or writing time.

Conversely, similar to Jack being able to work for long periods of time with blocks, children who struggle with inhibitory control but who have good spatial skills may be able to spend relatively longer if the activity draws on those skills they already have.

It is most important for teachers to devote extra attention to children who have both low self-control and low visuo-motor integration. These children's nascent visuo-motor integration skills mean they may have difficulty organizing their materials and completing tasks, and their weak self-control means they may have trouble persisting through frustration. Teachers can help guide them through activities and provide *other-regulation* until children's skills develop adequately and they can regulate themselves to complete tasks (Kopp, 1982).

SUMMARY

In the example below, targeting motor skills confers later benefits in EF and social-emotional domains—which then circle back to positively influence Alicia's motor skills. This is an example of a multiplying effect of the initial motor skills intervention. If the same intervention had been tried a few years later, however, Alicia might not have been willing to participate at all, which shows the importance of the timing of certain events during a child's life (Thelen, 2005).

In the next chapter, I explain how children's foundational cognitive skills contribute to their school readiness in literacy.

What About Alicia?

Thinking about Alicia, her poor motor skills may irritate her mother, especially when Alicia plays games with her 2-year-old brother, which usually leads to fighting. But then, her mother gives permission for Alicia to participate in a study at her preschool where the researchers attempt to improve motor skills, and Alicia is one of the children for whom the intervention works.

Alicia's mother notices her daughter's improved mindset about going to school, and this changes their relationship for the better. In turn, her mother decides to play games more often with both of her children. With her mother's help, Alicia develops greater appreciation for taking turns, more awareness of her little brother's needs, and more confidence about trying new activities both at school and at home. Her willingness to try new things leads her into a wider variety of social situations at recess, where she has the opportunity to refine her motor skills further.

CHAPTER 7

Literacy and the Theory of Automaticity

The twins Michael and Charlie have an older sister, Simone, who has loved books since she was an infant. Their mother began reading to her when she was just a few weeks old, and Simone learned how to turn pages in her board books years before she understood the connection between the letter symbols and the words her mother said. In preschool, her favorite activity was book reading, whether it was during circle time or cozied up on the beanbag with her favorite aide, Ms. Marla. During pretend play, Simone would "write" her own books and then "read" them to a friend.

Simone couldn't wait to learn to read, and when literacy instruction finally began, she was so familiar with the letter forms that it wasn't nearly as difficult as she thought it might be to learn the sounds they go with. Even though she had to work to keep all the different sounds in her mind when sounding out a word, she learned the pairings relatively quickly, because she and the twins' grandmother practiced every afternoon after school.

Simone also got lots of practice with writing utensils with a home full of not only books, but also art supplies, including crayons, markers, and colored pencils. Still, Simone's literacy progress is impeded by difficulties in learning to write. Some shapes are tricky because they are so similar, like b and d—both have round "o" and a straight-up line. And her kindergarten teacher, Mrs. Lowden, expects the children to sit at a small desk or table when they practice writing their letters; at home, Simone can lie on the floor to do her art. At school, she has trouble keeping her body pointed straight ahead; it feels more comfortable to turn her knees to the right so the left side of her body faces the desk. Then she can keep both hands on the left side of her body to write. But Mrs. Lowden insists that Simone face forward.

Soon Simone begins to dread alphabet-writing time and can hardly accomplish anything because she is so worried about her teacher noticing that her body is pointed the wrong way, but it feels so uncomfortable the way she is supposed to do it. The situation goes on long enough that the school psychologist recommends some sessions with an occupational therapist.

In this chapter, I explain how children draw on foundational cognitive skills during the process of literacy acquisition. There are several well-known connections between executive function and literacy, but motor skills and spatial skills also have their place.

In literacy, certain foundational cognitive skills or their components are more closely tied to certain literacy skills than others. So it is important to "look under the hood" of a broad concept like literacy and consider all the different cognitive processes that make reading and writing possible.

For example, the National Reading Panel (NRP) defines literacy as including the skills of phonics; phonological awareness; oral language, including receptive and expressive vocabulary; print knowledge, including emergent writing; and comprehension (NRP, 2000). The vignette about Simone divides literacy skills into *decoding*, or matching letter symbols to their sounds, and *emergent writing*, or forming written language with a writing utensil.

In this chapter, I explain how EF is especially important for decoding, whereas motor and spatial skills are implicated in emergent writing and vocabulary learning. I end by describing how the theory of automaticity helps explain how foundational cognitive skills connect with certain literacy processes.

> **THEME:** Executive function operates whenever we learn something new, but "shuts off" when we have learned or automated the skill (*theory of automaticity*). So EF is strongly connected to any new skills children are learning, including literacy. Physical experiences with the materials of reading (books and writing utensils), new concepts, and practicing reading and writing to automaticity also support literacy acquisition and rely on motor and spatial skills along with EF.

HOW EXECUTIVE FUNCTION SUPPORTS LITERACY ACQUISITION

As any teacher who has worked with a prereader knows, reading is not a natural act. Letter forms are made of arbitrary shapes, and those arbitrary shapes represent arbitrary sounds, which often change depending on the context of other letters around them. For example, think about the sound that the letter *g* makes in the word *giraffe* versus in the word *gorilla*.

To learn these various connections, both between letter shapes and sounds and between the written word and the meaning, takes intentional and deliberate work that includes memorization. Here is where executive function becomes critical, because children must *inhibit* incorrect sounds and meanings, use their *auditory working memory* to decode the sounds of individual letters and put them together to comprehend, and *shift* flexibly their interpretations of particular letter sounds depending on the context in which the letters appear.

Research across a range of samples demonstrates that children who walk into the early childhood classroom with strong EF also have better entering literacy skills and make better literacy progress over time (Blair, Protzko, & Ursache, 2011; Blair & Razza, 2007; McClelland et al., 2014). This association, between EF measured early and vocabulary and decoding outcomes measured later, holds for children of preschool age (4- to 5-year-olds) (McClelland, Cameron, Connor, et al., 2007) and kindergarten age (5- to 6-year-olds) (Cameron Ponitz, McClelland, Matthews, & Morrison, 2009).

Much research on EF and literacy is based on correlational studies, which makes it difficult to know which comes first and which should be emphasized in school readiness. Efforts to disentangle the direction of association suggest that EF precedes literacy, rather than vice versa (Fuhs, Nesbitt, Farran, & Dong, 2014).

In other words, it seems more important for a child to begin school with good EF than good reading skills, because if children have good EF skills, they can readily engage in the available opportunities to learn to read. For better or worse, much of classroom life depends on behavior as well as academics, which in early elementary school focuses on literacy. So children who can self-regulate their behaviors to engage in the learning opportunities provided will thrive. In one large study of almost 17,000 kindergartners, girls' better teacher-rated behaviors drawing on EF such as attention and persistence explained two-thirds of their advantage over boys in a composite reading test (Ready, LoGerfo, Burkam, & Lee, 2005).

Multiple studies have shown that children who have better overall EF, as well as individual components of EF, also have better literacy skills (Becker, Miao, Duncan, & McClelland, 2014; Blair & Razza, 2007; Cameron Ponitz, McClelland, et al., 2009; Fuhs et al., 2014; McClelland et al., 2014). I next explore how the individual components of EF are at work during literacy tasks.

Inhibitory Control and Multiple Literacy Skills

Recall that the process of inhibitory control means stopping an easy impulse in favor of a more difficult learned or planned behavior. This process is strongly linked to literacy success, even when other cognitive processes are accounted for in statistical models. For example, Becker et al. (2014) found that 4- and 5-year-olds with good inhibitory control also had better letter-word recognition and receptive vocabulary skills, even when accounting for auditory working memory, visuo-motor integration, and the HTKS task measuring overall EF. In another study of 125 4-year-olds, children's inhibitory control was related to their print knowledge but not their expressive vocabulary (Purpura, Schmitt, & Ganley, 2017).

In a separate study of 141 low-income children, Blair and Razza (2007) found that kindergartners with strong inhibitory control had better end-of-year letter knowledge and phonemic awareness. The study was powerful because it also controlled for cognitive flexibility and IQ, plus children's understanding that other people have different thoughts from those of the children themselves (*theory of mind*).

In a similar pattern, my colleagues and I found that a diverse group of 4-year-olds ($N = 467$) from five U.S. states who had strong preschool-entry inhibitory control skills had better print knowledge and phonological awareness at the end of the year (Cameron, Brock, et al., 2015). Inhibitory control was not related to children's vocabulary learning, measured either receptively (how many words they understand) or expressively (how many words they can produce).

EXECUTIVE FUNCTION AND EBOOKS DURING EARLY CHILDHOOD

There is growing research on computer and digital supports such as ebooks for children's literacy development. As with other school-readiness skills, how the tool is designed and how it is used are critical factors in whether it is a distraction or a benefit (Bus, Takacs, & Kegel, 2015).

In their review of ebook studies with children ages 3 to 6, Bus et al. (2015) report that when ebook animations and interactive features *match and enhance the story* versus add distracting sounds, "hot spot" activities, or unrelated images, children's comprehension can improve. Positive associations for well-designed ebooks appear most prevalent for children who otherwise find it difficult to sit still and focus during a traditional book reading.

Because children must resist the temptation to touch the device and distract themselves from the reading, some experts suggest that ebook readings with young children may be more successful if the teacher controls actions such as page turning and selecting sounds and other features (Roskos & Burstein, 2013). But when they are not allowed to touch the book, children are not given the chance to practice tactile skills or engage in text-based interactions that are usually involved in reading, whether traditional or ebooks.

In sum, there is early evidence to support both sides of the ebook vs. print book argument. This area of research is new and much remains unknown, and experts hope that future developments will reveal more specific recommendations based on ebook features and formats, and individual characteristics of children for whom ebooks are likely to work best.

These patterns suggest that inhibitory control can be considered a foundational cognitive skill for several aspects of literacy, especially tasks involving print as opposed to vocabulary (Purpura et al., 2017). Inhibitory control is needed when a skill is being acquired, or when learning is still effortful and not yet automatic (Blair et al., 2011). Inhibitory control keeps children on task and enables them to engage in the repeated exposures to letter and sound connections that support learning to read.

Working Memory and Phonological Awareness

In our study of 4-year-olds' school-readiness skills where we assessed inhibitory control and visuo-motor integration, my colleagues and I also had access to a direct assessment of children's working memory for letters and numbers (Cameron, Brock, et al., 2015).

> **EXERCISE:** For a sense of how a working memory assessment works, try the following, *without writing anything down*:
> » First, recall your parents' and your birthdays.
> » Now, reorder each number in those birthdays from smallest to largest.

For young children, the working memory assessment we used is not as difficult as this exercise, but the basic idea is the same: Children were asked to remember numbers and to rearrange them in reverse order. In other words, children were asked to do some "work" on the numbers while remembering (the "working" part of working memory).

We found that children with good working memory improved in phonological awareness skills over the year, but their working memory did not predict gains in vocabulary or print knowledge. This finding is consistent with a study of 125 4-year-olds that measured all three EF components and several literacy skills (Purpura et al., 2017). Children with good working memory had better phonological awareness, but working memory was not related to their vocabulary or print knowledge.

Phonological awareness means holding multiple pieces of information in mind, such as the sounds for *c*, *a*, and *t*, and combining them into the word *cat*. Especially before age 7, other literacy skills, such as vocabulary, draw from short-term memory, rather than working memory (Baddeley, Gathercole, & Papagno, 1998).

Cognitive Flexibility and Print Knowledge

Finally, children use cognitive flexibility to apply different rules for behavior and to switch between these rules. Recall from Chapter 3 that one thing that makes cognitive flexibility so challenging is that it usually requires inhibitory control as well (Diamond, Kirkham, & Amso, 2002).

For example, two friends may use their own set of made-up rules for a letter-matching game—perhaps they match the letters with a round element (*a*, *b*, *d*, *g*, and so on). When a new child joins the game and an aide encourages them to use the game's official rules, matching small and uppercase letters, the two friends must not only remember the new rules, but ignore the old rules.

Purpura et al. (2017) found that children with better cognitive flexibility also had better print knowledge, but cognitive flexibility didn't matter for children's vocabulary or phonological awareness after controlling for inhibitory control and phonological working memory. Somewhat similarly, Blair and Razza (2007) found that cognitive flexibility only predicted children's literacy skills until inhibitory control was accounted for.

Based on these studies, the reason that young children's cognitive flexibility predicts their literacy outcomes may be largely because of inhibitory control. Still, Purpura et al. (2017) found that both inhibitory control and cognitive flexibility were unique predictors of print knowledge, which they attributed to children having to "shift between using names and sounds (sometimes different sounds) as appropriate" (p. 30).

Similar to Blair and Razza's (2007) conclusion, these results suggest that children need cognitive flexibility the most during the finite period of time when they are learning to associate letter forms and letter sounds. After that point, they continue to need inhibitory control, to sit still and practice their literacy skills to achieve fluency.

MOTOR AND SPATIAL SKILLS USED IN LITERACY

Children must automate not just their decoding skills, but the motor skills they use in literacy tasks. Turning pages, handling paper and writing utensils, and writing smoothly are all complex motor sequences that rely on both gross and fine motor skills (see also Chapter 4). Specific tasks include turning pages while reading and holding a marker or pencil with one hand and the writing surface with the nonwriting hand. *Graphomotor skills* are those skills needed to wield a writing utensil, whether for handwriting or drawing.

Gross and Fine Motor Foundations of Literacy

First, children must be able to sit comfortably and remain stable while manipulating pages or a writing utensil and paper. Another gross motor concept, bilateral integration, also called "crossing the midline" (see Chapter 4), is important for fluent writing because writing posture assumes children will have the paper in front of them and, in the English language, write from left to right (Beery & Beery, 2010).

Beery and Beery (2010) suggest that children will have success in learning to write when they can make the plus symbol (+). This symbol is involved in making many letters and requires crossing the midline: bringing the writing utensil toward the body, then switching mid-stroke to bring it away from the body.

Like Simone in the opening vignette, children who resist crossing the midline may turn their bodies to one side so they can keep the paper and writing utensil on the opposite side. They may also switch the pencil from one hand to another in the middle of a task, or use their right hand for right-sided tasks and their left hand for left-sided tasks (Kid Sense Child Development Corporation, 2017). Although these behaviors may not prevent children from writing, awkward posture preferences may interfere with children being able to write for long periods, and could bother those sitting around them.

> *EXERCISE:* Imagine trying to read a book or write a letter while working on an exercise machine such as a stair climber or elliptical machine. This challenge to an adult's balance and coordination is similar to the challenge that children new to literacy activities may experience in their motor skills when trying to sit upright to read or write.

Motor Skills and Handwriting

In an article summarizing themes from research on writing, Feder and Majnemer (2007) listed the "performance components" of handwriting (p. 313), which implicate each of the foundational cognitive skills in this book—but especially motor skills. The following list includes four components related to motor skills that are not discussed elsewhere in this chapter:

Sensory modalities: Another term for the senses. Handwriting draws directly on the visual and tactile senses. Children with sensory sensitivities may avoid handwriting tasks. On the other hand, children whose fingers don't provide them with enough information may overrely on visual cues during handwriting, which leads to fatigue.

Proprioception: Though not a motor skill, proprioception or kinesthesia refers to the awareness of one's body or body parts in space (see Chapter 4). Applied to handwriting, this sense guides the pencil grip and writing pressure, as well as the direction of the writing utensil.

In-hand manipulation: In-hand manipulation means handling objects after grasping them; applied to handwriting, this means the writing utensil. It includes *translation* (moving the object between fingers and palm) and *rotation* (rolling the object in the fingers), not to be confused with the spatial skill of transformation-rotation defined in Chapter 5.

Motor planning: Motor planning, or praxis, is a complex skill that involves several subconscious processes as well as EF when children evaluate their performance and set goals (Willingham, 1998). It includes isolation, timing, sequencing, and grading of movements.

Consistent with the range of skills listed here are other studies indicating that handwriting is a complex task that draws on basic motor skills along with more advanced cognitive skills. Virginia Berninger of the University of Washington and colleagues (1992) conducted a study to understand the different developmental subskills that underlie handwriting. Many of the tasks they asked children to perform may not seem related to handwriting, yet they show surprising connections.

The researchers found that of four tasks that explained two-thirds of the differences in the handwriting performance of 300 1st-, 2nd-, and 3rd-graders, one was a basic motor task called *finger succession* (Berninger et al., 1992). In finger succession, the child "touched the thumb with each finger, in sequential order, beginning with the little finger and moving to the index finger, as quickly as possible until told to stop (after 5 cycles)" (p. 262). Children performed the task with each hand, without looking.

Of note, several other basic fine motor tasks, including *finger repetition* (tapping the index finger as fast as possible) and *finger lifting* (isolating the movement of a single finger), were not related to handwriting. These results are consistent with a distinction noted in Chapter 4. Considering types of motor skills that support handwriting, it is more important for children to produce *sequenced* movements quickly than *repetitive* movements quickly. This is because fluent, accurate handwriting requires complex motor planning of multiple movements that must be appropriately timed and organized to produce legible writing.

Spatial Skills and Handwriting

Most recent studies claiming to connect fine motor skills with literacy have actually been using a direct assessment of spatial skills, visuo-motor integration. In Chapter 5, I wrote about visuo-motor integration as a constructional task. Handwriting is a very specific constructional task: Children reproduce letters by either copying letter forms they see on the board, worksheet, or cards, or by referring to an image in their mind.

The constructional similarities between copying tasks and handwriting help explain connections between visuo-motor integration and literacy outcomes. Recall that in preschool, children with good visuo-motor integration also have better print knowledge (Cameron, Brock, et al., 2015). Additionally, school-age children who do well on form-copying tasks like the Beery VMI also have better letter-word identification, print knowledge, and phonological awareness (Cameron, Brock, et al., 2012); handwriting (Ho, 2011); and writing in general (Carlson, Rowe, & Curby, 2013).

It turns out that handwriting is even more complex than traditional copying tasks. Furthermore, when researchers are able to measure constructional tasks that involve children writing or copying letters or words using the alphabet, these tasks prove to be more aligned with handwriting outcomes than the ability to copy abstract designs on the VMI (Berninger et al., 1992). Being able to reproduce the letters of the alphabet quickly and clearly is a strong predictor of writing outcomes in 2nd and 6th grade (Medwell, Strand, & Wray, 2007, 2009).

Emerging Support for Embodied Vocabulary and Comprehension

The last link between motor skills and literacy acquisition that I want to introduce is emerging support for how movement contributes to the development of vocabulary and comprehension in early childhood. Recall from Chapter 4 that the idea of "embodied cognition" acknowledges that learning happens while we are in our physical bodies. *Embodiment* assumes that our physical actions in that environment both provide a context for and facilitate that learning.

You may be familiar with the idea that vocabulary words are easier to learn when we experience them in multiple modalities. For example, if children sing a song about a blue heron, see a photo of a blue heron, draw a picture of it, and act out the bird's behavior in the wild, they will remember the concept of "blue heron" better than if they simply learn the word *heron* paired with a picture. The learning advantage arises because all the different instances and experiences of a blue heron represent multiple ways of *encoding* the information in the child's mind.

Learning about a concept in multiple sensory modalities also increases the possibility that children will make connections between the new information and their prior knowledge and experience. For example, when singing "Row, Row, Row Your Boat," a child remembers a canoe ride when they watched large water birds fly across the stream.

Researchers at Arizona State University have been studying another way to see whether children who embody certain concepts by acting them out *encode* (another way to say *learn*) them better. They found that in a book-reading situation tested in the laboratory, children who acted out parts of the story using farm animal toys remembered the text better than children who had only reread the story (Glenberg, Gutierrez, Levin, Japuntich, & Kaschak, 2004). Interestingly, the acting-out strategy worked even when children simply *imagined* carrying out the actions.

In a follow-up study, the embodied book reading successfully improved comprehension when it was carried out in three-person groups of children ages 6 to 8, suggesting the activity's appropriateness for use in classroom small-group settings (Glenberg, Brown, & Levin, 2007). Other related research, though nascent, suggests that acting out the physical actions of a story, as well as adopting the emotions and personality traits of characters in the story, can be effective for improving story comprehension (Berenhaus, Oakhill, & Rusted, 2015).

To act out a story, children certainly use their motor skills, but even thinking about moving may help children learn new words. One study of 76 German preschoolers examined children's understanding of general vocabulary words like *sky* and "body-object interaction" vocabulary words, which are words like *feather* and *spoon*, where there is an easy-to-imagine possibility for bodily action applied to the object the word represents (Suggate & Stoeger, 2014). The researchers also measured fine motor skills with pegboard completion, bead threading, and block turning.

Results showed that to the extent that children's fine motor skills were related to general vocabulary, it was because children with better fine motor skills scored higher on the body-object interaction words. The authors concluded that studies reporting no associations between fine motor skills and vocabulary development failed to consider body-object interaction possibilities in the word choices offered in the vocabulary tests.

These results support the *embodied cognition hypothesis*. As applied to vocabulary and comprehension development, this hypothesis states that words that can be acted upon using a physical movement should be easier to learn than concepts that can't be acted upon.

Specifically, embodying a word or sequence in a story is thought to promote efficient encoding because acting out the concept creates an accessible mental "index" for children that they can refer to later. That is, acting out a previously abstract idea gives the concept meaning to a child that it didn't have before (Berenhaus et al., 2015; Glenberg et al., 2004). And when children need to recall the idea later to comprehend its meaning, it doesn't take them as long to retrieve that memory (that is, recall is faster), because they created an easy-to-remember index by acting out the idea.

There is some debate about the reach of this hypothesis—for example, if all learning must be embodied, then how do humans comprehend abstract concepts such as free will, peace, or integrity? Still, the findings that have emerged in favor of this hypothesis in early childhood are intriguing and worth following in the future.

HOW THE THEORY OF AUTOMATICITY CONNECTS
FOUNDATIONAL COGNITIVE SKILLS WITH READING AND WRITING

At the beginning of this chapter, I described how each EF component plays a special role for at least one literacy skill. So it is not surprising that EF assessments like the HTKS, which require all three components of inhibitory control, working memory, and cognitive flexibility, are robust predictors of diverse literacy outcomes (Cameron, Brock, et al., 2012; McClelland et al., 2014).

A concept called automaticity theory helps explain these research results further. In reading specifically, the concept of automaticity is referred to as *fluency*. This means that a reader doesn't have to think about the individual sounds of letters or the meaning of individual words. Instead, the reader has learned to recognize letters of words automatically.

But how does a reader become fluent? In the context of learning to read, children must rehearse facts (such as the letter *d* makes the /d/ sound), literacy symbols (such as knowing a half-circle with a line to its right is the letter *d*), and motor routines such as turning a page so they can be carried out smoothly, without deliberate attention. And the only way to become a smooth performer of all these routines is through deliberate, nonautomatic practice (Floyer-Lea & Matthews, 2004).

EF is critical in helping children focus their attention and delay the impulse to leave the task to do something easier and more fun. EF, specifically working memory, helps children access and manipulate any knowledge they have that is relevant to making meaning from what they are reading—such as vocabulary words or prior experiences that support comprehension.

Executive function is also needed to learn the fundamental motor routines of the early childhood classroom, which then frees up their cognitive resources for learning more complex tasks. For example, children must learn to sit still, handle a book, and turn pages before they can focus their attention on the content of the pages. For children to become fluent in handwriting, they need EF to focus their attention on holding the writing utensil and paper, and avoid distractions.

In other words, just as children become fluent decoders through a lot of practice, handwriting also improves through deliberate practice to create automaticity (Medwell & Wray, 2014). And early in this developmental process, children devote significant cognitive resources to carry out more basic skills, including motor skills, such as managing the pencil and forming letters.

After children spend enough time mastering the basic skills, they can then turn their attention to higher-level learning goals. Unfortunately, research suggests that well after early childhood—as late as 6th grade—21% of the quality in youth's compositions is the result of how legibly they can write individual alphabet letters on a measure called the Alphabet Task (Medwell et al., 2009). In the authors' words:

> The Alphabet Task measures the mental generation and motor production of the letter symbols . . . automatic performance at this orthographic–motor integration [task] . . . frees up the working memory to focus on composing. (p. 335)

Just as it helps explain how children learn to decode fluently, automaticity theory explains how individuals become faster at the motor routines of handwriting by practicing them over and over.

SUMMARY

Children need each of the foundational cognitive skills to learn to read and write. The EF component of inhibitory control helps children ignore tempting distractions to focus on the difficult tasks of turning letter symbols into words and making meaningful and legible marks on a page with a pencil. Working memory helps them notice and combine the individual sounds of letters into words. And cognitive flexibility helps children identify the correct sound of a given letter in the context of a certain word, or similarly, to decide on the correct meaning of a given word in the context of a particular sentence.

Gross motor skills support good book reading, and proper writing posture and fine motor skills make for effective interactions with print materials, including books and the tools of writing. Reproducing letters of the alphabet (handwriting) can be thought of as a spatial skill, specifically a constructional task, and students who can write the alphabet well are better writers. Finally, children may find it easier to learn vocabulary and comprehension skills when they use their motor skills to act out words or scenes.

Automaticity theory helps explain some of these links. This theory states that when children practice a skill enough times, the skill becomes automatic, or fluent. Applied to literacy acquisition, children who practice enough to become fluent in holding books, decoding, and writing benefit from having cognitive resources freed to devote to other higher-order tasks.

What About Simone?

Simone's occupational therapist recommends some games to help her practice the skills that she needs before she will be able to enjoy emergent writing time. Simone gets a kick out of their sessions spent acting like a windmill, touching one foot with the opposite hand; closing her eyes and touching her nose; playing Twister; and playing other games where she has to cross her body with her arms, hands, or feet. The therapist also has her do some writing exercises set to music—but she doesn't make letters, just shapes like the sails of a boat or the wings of flying birds.

Simone enjoys the routines so much that she goes home and teaches them to her twin brothers, Michael and Charlie. After about 8 weeks, Simone's teacher, Mrs. Lowden, realizes she doesn't have to fight with Simone when it's emergent writing time. Simone's writing is not the most beautiful in the class, but it's legible, and more important, Simone is willing to engage in the process.

CHAPTER 8

Mathematics Skills Develop Together with Foundational Cognitive Skills

Four-year-old Miriam loves playing tabletop games. She adores the game pieces and the colorful boards or play surfaces. Her favorite are the dice—the more of those white cubes with black dots she can find, the better. Often, you find Miriam rolling dice in a cup and pretending to count the dots. But you notice that she doesn't count accurately, and instead just recites numbers while rolling the dice in her hand.

Inaccurate counting also happens when you engage Miriam in the Chutes and Ladders board game. You don't mind her mistakes when counting, but the other children do! You wonder if Miriam will just outgrow this tendency to ignore the units she is counting, or if you should correct the errors more often. You have read that "children learn through play," and you don't want to turn game time into teacher-directed instruction.

The dice and board games that Miriam enjoys are examples of *informal math* activities. In this chapter, I describe the role of the foundational cognitive skills in the different processes that children use when they learn and do mathematics. These processes have specific associations with the foundational cognitive skills (Purpura et al., 2017). I end this chapter by describing two successful interventions that improve math skills in early childhood.

Three types of mathematics processes are linked to three distinct, underlying brain networks that encode and process:

Auditory verbal knowledge used for rote math facts and number skills
Nonverbal knowledge such as the number line and knowledge used in geometry
The visual Arabic code used to identify and spatially manipulate numbers and quantities in the symbolic (that is, the Arabic numeral) format (Dehaene, 1992; LeFevre et al., 2010)

Despite progress in breaking down math into these separable processes, most of the research that links foundational cognitive skills with quantitative skills in early childhood represents and assesses math as a single broad skill. The skill that receives the most emphasis corresponds to the first item on the list above, verbal knowledge of numbers. This means that in general, in research among young children, studies have tended to overlook both the nonverbal and especially spatial aspects of children's knowledge about math (Clements & Sarama, 2011). Yet, to understand the role of foundational cognitive skills for a given quantitative task, it helps to consider what type of math process the task taps (LeFevre et al., 2010).

> **THEME:** Like reading, learning different mathematics skills is challenging and involves EF. Acquiring automaticity (for example, automating the times tables) enables children to advance to more complex concepts. Spatial skills are also closely linked to mathematics, which explains why some interventions that improve children's math achievement also improve their spatial skills.

EXECUTIVE FUNCTION AND MATHEMATICS

In the previous chapter, I emphasized that when children are first learning to read, they use executive function to decode the sounds of letters, knit them into words, and put them in the context of the sentence. Later, children use EF to comprehend sentences and put them in the context of paragraphs and larger text units.

Both literacy and mathematics rely on symbols—either alphabetic or numeric—that children must learn to recognize and turn into meaning, and then interpret within a particular context (Cameron, Grimm, Steele, Castro-Schilo, & Grissmer, 2015; LeFevre et al., 2010). So in some ways, the role of EF in mathematics is similar to the role that EF plays in reading, especially when children are first learning math.

The Role of EF When Children Are First Learning Math

Two unrelated studies that asked how much of children's EF is involved in their math achievement found remarkably similar results, despite involving very different samples. Math skills were measured in both studies with different types of counting tasks as well as general number knowledge.

The first study was conducted with 115 5- to 7-year-olds in the Netherlands (Kroesbergen, Van Luit, Van Lieshout, Van Loosbroek, & Van de Rijt, 2009). Children's EF was measured with three tasks: a direct assessment of planning, where they had to move pegs to copy a model in as few steps as possible; a working memory task, where they had to remember lists of numbers in the reverse order; and an inhibitory control task, where they had to ignore the size of a pictured animal and state the real-life size of the animal.

The second study was conducted with 44 3- to 4-year-olds from two states in the northeastern United States (Verdine, Irwin, Golinkoff, & Hirsh-Pasek, 2014). Children's EF was measured with two tasks: an inhibitory control task, where they had to refrain from imitating the examiner who tapped a dowel either once or twice; and a cognitive flexibility task, where they had to find two similar pictures based on varying traits—shape, size, or color.

Both studies found that just over 40% (45% in the first study, and 43% in the second study) of children's scores on a general mathematics test could be explained by knowing their EF task scores. These two studies add to an established body of research that shows that children's math skills are robustly linked to their EF skills in the school transition years (Cameron, Brock, et al., 2012).

In different samples, and controlling for language, SES, and other variables such as IQ, children's EF at the beginning of a school year—whether preschool or kindergarten—also accounts for gains in their math skills over the year (Cameron Ponitz, McClelland, et al., 2009; McClelland, Cameron, Connor, et al., 2007). There is related evidence that entering school with better EF helps children grow in math beyond that single year (Blair, Ursache, Greenberg, & Vernon-Feagans, 2015; McClelland et al., 2014). So EF plays a large role when children are first acquiring mathematics knowledge, but its role changes as children develop automaticity in certain number skills. This pattern may be familiar because a similar process occurs for literacy, described in Chapter 7.

Number Skills Can Be Automated, but Word Problems and Advanced Mathematics Always Require EF

For literacy, as children progress through early elementary school, EF becomes used for comprehension instead of decoding (Fuhs, Nesbitt, Farran, & Dong, 2014). That is, when children finally become fluent readers, they no longer need EF because they can quickly and easily focus their attention on the text, combine letters with sounds to make words (or recognize the words by sight), and inhibit incorrect words or quickly correct a word they've misread based on context.

In a similar pattern, it turns out that if children successfully automate certain skills—such as math facts and procedures—then the math tasks that rely on such automaticity also become easier over time.

In one study of 205 5- to 7-year-olds, having better number skills was associated with better calculation abilities (Fuchs et al., 2010); EF assessed with planning didn't make a difference. The authors explained this pattern by concluding that only number skills were needed for the calculation task. And because children had already automated their number skills, EF didn't play much of a role in their calculations.

This result makes sense if you consider how much practice children get in addition, subtraction, multiplication, and division during the early elementary years. With so much practice, most elementary students hardly need to think about or make a plan to solve simple calculation problems.

Other types of math, specifically word problems, continue to involve EF even when number and calculation skills have been automated (Fuchs et al., 2010). Word problems usually involve multiple concepts that implicate language, space, and quantity, in addition to number. Children need EF, especially working memory, to keep track of all these different types of information and combine them to solve the problem.

Finally, advancing in mathematics means constantly learning new symbols—such as going from + and − to ∞—and using cognitive flexibility to change the meaning of the symbols, depending on the problem context (Mix & Cheng, 2012). Realizing that abstract symbols can represent complex concepts takes place over the first years of early elementary school, described by experts as the 5 to 7 year shift (Case, 1996; Weisner, 1996). This impressive and dynamic process begins in a simple place: with concrete experiences that depend on motor skills.

MOTOR COORDINATION AND MATHEMATICS

The earliest known scholars of infant and child development—Jean Piaget, Maria Montessori, Friedrich Froebel, and Rudolf Steiner—all shared the insight that young children learn first with their eyes, bodies, and hands. "Hands on, minds on" learning is especially significant for learning mathematics, because classroom-based research suggests that manipulatives help children learn about number, space, and quantity at particular times in development (Guarino, Dieterle, Bargagliotti, & Mason, 2013).

Large-scale studies indicate that children's kindergarten-entry fine motor skills help explain how they do in 1st, 5th, and 8th grade in mathematics achievement assessed with a general test (Grissmer, Grimm, Aiyer, Murrah, & Steele, 2010; Murrah, 2010; Son & Meisels, 2006).

A growing number of follow-up studies points to visuo-motor integration—which I've categorized as part of spatial skills (see Chapter 5)—as the key process that is responsible for links with mathematics achievement (Carlson et al., 2013). I will get to that shortly—but in this section, I want to share some intriguing evidence that other skills involving motor processes, more basic than visuo-motor integration, also contribute to how children learn mathematics.

As graduate students at the University of Virginia, former teachers Helyn Kim and Chelsea Duran wondered whether more advanced skills, such as visuo-motor integration, build on the more basic skill of motor coordination, and how this may contribute to children's mathematics achievement.

I helped them answer this question using data collected with 135 5-year-olds (kindergartners) and 119 6-year-olds (1st-graders) on a series of projects led by David Grissmer (Kim, Duran, Cameron, & Grissmer, 2017). Our sample included a majority of African American children (71%) and a similar percentage of children whose families were from low-income backgrounds and from either Virginia or South Carolina. Like the matching results I shared earlier about EF-math links from the Netherlands and the northeastern United States, our findings from these two different states are more dependable than if they were from a single community.

Children's fine motor coordination was assessed with a task that required them to trace in between two narrow lines—similar to staying inside the lines in a coloring book. Visuo-motor integration was assessed with a design-copying measure very similar to the Beery VMI, and mathematics was assessed with a combination of three subtests of children's number skills, geometry, and measurement. An assessment of attention, requiring children to ignore distractors to focus on and circle with a pencil certain target symbols—such as a face or a cat—was also given as part of EF. I here focus on the results for the younger group of children, who were assessed three times: at the beginning of kindergarten, between kindergarten and 1st grade, and between 1st and 2nd grade.

The longitudinal study used the statistical analysis called *mediation* to control for background factors and attention. Results suggested (1) interdependence of spatial and math skills, and (2) a hierarchical pattern from motor to spatial to math. Specifically:

1. Early visuo-motor integration and mathematics skills contributed to each other later. Children who began kindergarten with strong visuo-motor integration learned more in math over the year, and children who began kindergarten with good math skills grew more in visuo-motor integration over the year. The same pattern emerged when looking from the end of kindergarten to the end of 1st grade: Children who began 1st grade with strong visuo-motor integration learned more math by the end of the year, and vice versa.

This finding is an example of interdependence of skill development. *Interdependence* refers to Esther Thelen's (2005) observation that development is like a complex system, where simple cause-effect associations are inappropriate because "the whole system is so mutually embedded and interdependent" (p. 259). Applied to school readiness, interdependence means that there is no single most important area of school readiness, and no single activity or skill that causes all the other skills to develop. Instead, skills develop alongside one another—called "co-development"—and improvements in one skill contribute to multiplying improvements in other skill areas (Kim et al., 2017).

2. Early kindergarten fine motor coordination was important for end-of-kindergarten visuo-motor integration, which in turn was important for 1st-grade mathematics. Also among kindergartners, even though their fine motor coordination did not directly matter for their future math skills, it mattered indirectly. This was because children who had relatively better fine motor coordination at the beginning of kindergarten had better visuo-motor integration at the end of kindergarten, which was then associated with having better mathematics scores at the end of 1st grade.

This finding shows how fine motor coordination is a foundation for visuo-motor integration: Drawing in between two narrow lines is easier than copying a symbol or design.

Figure 8.1 shows a simplified visual representation of these results for the end of kindergarten through the end of 1st grade, based on the more complex analysis reported in Kim et al. (2017).

- Notice how, at the beginning of kindergarten, the light gray box in the middle overlaps with the dark gray box on the right, and the arrows emanate up from where they meet. The placement of the arrows means that visuo-motor integration and math skills

Figure 8.1. Motor Coordination and Visuo-Motor Integration Are Early Foundations of Math Skills (adapted from Kim et al., 2017)

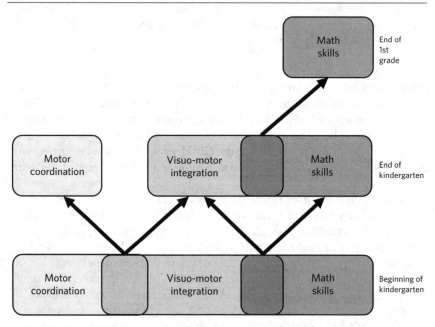

measured at the beginning of kindergarten both contribute to each other later, at the end of kindergarten.

- Notice how you can follow an arrow from fine motor coordination at the beginning of kindergarten (white box at the bottom left), to visuo-motor integration at the end of kindergarten (gray box in the middle), to math skills at the end of 1st grade (dark gray box at the top right). This finding also shows how math skills build on visuo-motor integration (which builds upon fine motor coordination).

Our study supports the theory that certain skills, including fine motor coordination, help form a foundation for the more complex skill of visuo-motor integration (a spatial skill), which in turn contributes to children's growth in mathematics (Case, 1996). Next, I explore in more depth the extent to which spatial skills are important for certain mathematics skills.

SPATIAL SKILLS AND DIFFERENT MATHEMATICS SKILLS

Math tasks that involve some type of spatial thinking include spatially representing and interpreting information about numbers. At the beginning of the early childhood period, around age 3, children begin to associate number words with quantitative and spatial concepts (Krajewski & Schneider, 2009), even as the three types of math knowledge I described earlier in this chapter remain distinct (LeFevre et al., 2010).

As a reminder, those three types are auditory verbal knowledge for number *words*, nonverbal knowledge for *magnitude* and the *number line*, and the visual Arabic code for numerical *symbols*. I don't have room here to describe the research in this area comprehensively, but the important thing to remember is that math is complex and made up of different types of knowledge. And, as children proceed through preschool and early elementary school, having strong spatial skills becomes an advantage for learning math (LeFevre et al., 2010). A long list of mathematics tasks relies on children's spatial skills, which include the following:

- The understanding of **one-to-one correspondence,** or assigning a unique number name to each object or unit when counting
- **Subitizing,** which means that children can look quickly at (visually perceive) a small set of objects and know the cardinal number automatically, without having to count
- Creating and referring to a mental image of the **number line,** an imaginary line organized from left to right, with negative numbers on the left, zero in the middle, and positive numbers on the right

- **_Estimating_** or making approximate calculations
- Solving **_geometry_** problems that entail position, space, patterns, and angles

In one study of 182 middle-SES 4- to 7-year-olds from Canada, children's spatial skills measured in either preschool or kindergarten played a role 2 years later in number skills, subitizing, the number line, and geometry. The only outcome with which spatial skills were not associated was a test that required children to say which number symbol represented a larger quantity (for example, "Is 5 or 15 bigger?") (LeFevre et al., 2010).

Other evidence suggests that spatial skills _are_ involved with other types of nonverbal representations, however (Kim & Cameron, 2016). These include perceiving, estimating, and performing transformations, which have been linked to adults' ability to compare magnitude with numbers represented in Arabic numbers or using a number line (Thompson, Nuerk, Moeller, & Cohen Kadosh, 2013). Mix and Cheng (2012) put it like this: "It would appear that people solve word problems and equations via the same cognitive processes that allow them to imagine a cube rotating" (p. 207).

Among children, there is a special role for spatial working memory in comparing or performing other mental operations involving magnitude or quantity (Kolkman, Kroesbergen, & Leseman, 2014). Children must perceive the "magnitude concept," and before performing an operation, it must be translated from symbol to quantity or vice versa; for instance, seeing five dots and thinking the word _five_, or seeing the symbol 5 and thinking of the concept of five units of something. Then to perform an operation such as a magnitude comparison, the first concept must be held in short-term memory while children think of the comparison concept (such as 3), and continue to use working memory to compare the two concepts and decide which is larger.

Spatial working memory is one explanation for why interventions that help children learn math also help children learn spatial skills (Cheng & Mix, 2014). This reiterates the close coupling between spatial skills and certain math skills (Mix & Cheng, 2012). But this doesn't mean that all spatial tasks are related to all mathematics tasks. In fact, correlations between spatial tasks and math performance vary widely, from around .10 (a weak correlation) to around .70 and above (a strong correlation).

Positive correlations range from 0 (no correlation) to 1 (perfect correlation) and represent how closely related two variables are to each other. The value of 1 represents a variable's correlation with itself, and the closer the correlation value is to 1, the more similar two separate variables are. Multiplying a correlation value by itself tells the percentage of the variability in the first variable that can be explained by knowing the second variable.

A correlation of .10 means that knowing a child's spatial task score explains only .10 times .10, or 1% of the math task score. On the other hand, a correlation of .70 means that knowing the spatial task score explains .7 times .7, or 49% of the math task score. One percent versus 49% is a big difference, and means that educators need to look closely to best understand which types of spatial tasks are most related to particular math skills. A dearth of research in this area among young children limits the extent to which scientific evidence can guide early childhood practice (Mix & Cheng, 2012).

Even so, results continue to emerge reiterating the importance of constructional skills. For example, among 44 3- to 5-year-old children from the Northeast United States, having strong visuo-motor integration and spatial assembly skills explained about 45% of their scores on a test of number knowledge (identification, counting, magnitude) (Verdine et al., 2014). In this sample, spatial skills explained about as much in number knowledge as did children's vocabulary and their SES.

In the next section, I describe how a successful mathematics intervention called Building Blocks helps children practice and develop their transformational and constructional skills, with positive results for geometry as well as counting and related number skills. I also describe the Linear Number Board Game, which helps children acquire counting and number line skills.

INTERVENTIONS THAT SHOWCASE THE CONNECTION BETWEEN SPATIAL AND MATHEMATICS SKILLS

I want to highlight a message that Mix and Cheng wrote in their widely cited 2012 chapter: Special types of movement through space appear to be one common thread in the diverse set of interventions to improve spatial or math skills among children. They note, "This is quite interesting from an embodiment standpoint because it suggests that it is not only space but *movement through space* that helps children learn" (Mix & Cheng, 2012, p. 230, emphasis added).

This pro-movement message aligns with popular philosophies about developmentally appropriate early childhood education. At the same time, this claim needs to be tested empirically to see *which types* of movement, actions, or activities help the most for learning particular concepts. Here are two mathematics interventions that show promise for improving spatial skills as well as math performance in young children.

The Building Blocks™ Curriculum

Doug Clements and Julie Sarama, professors at the University of Denver, are experts in early childhood mathematics learning and mathematics education, respectively. They believe that except for simple calculations, mathematics is all about spatial thinking. They write, "Mathematics is a special kind of language through which we communicate ideas that are essential-ly spatial" (Clements & Sarama, 2011, p. 134). While professors at the University at Buffalo, they created the Building Blocks curriculum for young children, which is based on two "building blocks" of mathematics compe-tence: spatial skills and number skills (Clements & Sarama, 2007).

In education research, strong claims like the one I am about to state are rare, but the 5-month Building Blocks curriculum definitively causes preschool-age children to learn more math than children who are exposed to other activities. Evidence comes from multiple randomized-to-treatment-or-control experiments with large samples of children (Clements, Sarama, Spitler, Lange, & Wolfe, 2011; Klein, Starkey, Clements, Sarama, & Iyer, 2008).

Building Blocks uses software, manipulatives, and pencil-and-paper ac-tivities to structure specific experiences that allow children to progress from novice to more expert in their understanding of geometry and number skills. Much of the work by Clements and Sarama and their colleagues has been to create a "learning progression," which describes the levels of understanding through which children pass when they move from novice to more expert in a given area of math.

Because of my focus on spatial skills, in this chapter, I highlight the ge-ometry part of the curriculum. Geometry relies heavily on spatial skills, in-cluding transformations, which are based on being able to recognize shapes from their features and to create complex shapes from pieces. Geometry is underemphasized in early childhood teacher education programs, another reason to highlight it here (Clements & Sarama, 2011).

The Building Blocks curriculum shows particularly strong effects for preschoolers' skills with shapes (Clements et al., 2011). The skill of *shape composition* means that children can piece together multiple smaller shapes to create a single, more complex, composite shape; it's related to within-ob-ject spatial skills and spatial assembly skills (see Chapter 5). Researchers watched young children working with materials and used their observations to create the following simplified learning progression for shape composi-tion (Clements, Wilson, & Sarama, 2004). A child

1. Uses individual shapes as individual objects, can't create the composite shape out of smaller shapes;
2. Is able to combine some shapes accurately using trial and error;
3. Is able to combine some shapes on purpose, using their attributes—for example, "I need one with a long side"; and
4. Creates composite shapes from multiple sets of smaller shapes.

Based on this learning progression, the curriculum has children work with individual shapes on and off the computer on increasingly complex instructional tasks, such as creating outlines of smaller shapes. Tasks are designed to help children practice in the next level of understanding, based on where they start. Therefore, the curriculum includes the following:

- Individualized tasks
- Working with engaging visuals and materials
- Structured and supported activity

Building Blocks curriculum activities tend to be game- or play-based, can include appropriate video and computer activities, and are structured experiences where a more able adult engages with children in playing and giving feedback aligned with the learning goals. Many of these features also appear in the next intervention and bolster my take-home message about guided object play that I further develop in Chapters 9 and 10.

The Linear Number Board Game

Another exciting early mathematics intervention is the Linear Number Board Game research conceptualized by Geetha Ramani of the University of Maryland and Robert Siegler of Carnegie Mellon University (2008, 2011). Although they aimed to improve math skills during early childhood, their work implicates spatial skills, too.

Ramani and Siegler (2008) designed a board game to teach children from low-income backgrounds that numbers progress linearly as you count up or down in integers. The board game is set up similar to Chutes and Ladders, with numbered squares arranged in a grid. The goal is to reach the "end" first, and a turn consists of spinning a spinner or rolling a die and advancing one's game piece the number of squares shown on the spinner or die.

Compared to children in a control group who played alternate layouts of the game using either a grid with colored squares or a circular version, children who play the board game with numbers on the squares improve in several skills. After several studies to determine why only the numbered grid version of the board game "works," spatial skills emerge as critical for two reasons:

1. Children who play using a circular board instead of a grid do not show the same improvements in number skills as children who play with a grid (Siegler & Ramani, 2009). The researchers suspect that a grid arrangement helps children internalize the spacing between numbers that are far apart. In their words, "Linear representations of numerical magnitudes seem likely to help children learn arithmetic because such *representations maintain equal subjective spacing* throughout the entire range of numbers, thus facilitating discrimination among answers to different problems" (p. 548, emphasis added).

2. Children who start their turn by "counting-on"—that is, counting with the actual numbers on the board (for example, counting "7, 8, 9" when they roll a 3 and begin from square 6), **improve, but children who start their turn by starting over at 1 do not** (e.g., counting "1, 2, 3" in the same scenario).

Evidence suggests that children's mental image of the number grid becomes more accurate when they play the game using the count-on procedure, but not when they begin over again from 1 on each turn (Laski & Siegler, 2014). Teachers should correct children's errors when they play, and this type of feedback is something that paraprofessionals working in Head Start classrooms can easily do when playing the game with their children (Ramani, Siegler, & Hitti, 2012).

In sum, the Linear Number Board Game helps children learn one-to-one correspondence between number names and single squares (units) on the grid, and to understand that the distance between individual integers is the same (1 unit). Finally, the game may support children developing the awareness that larger integers are a farther distance from zero than smaller units.

Similar to how ebooks *may* be helpful for literacy—depending on their unique features—*how* teachers support children's learning during both Building Blocks activities and Linear Number Board game play matters, which I expand on next.

ALIGNING ACTIVITIES WITH LEARNING GOALS

Taken together, years of research on the successful Building Blocks and the Linear Number Board Game illustrate the interconnectedness of spatial skills with activities that explicitly target mathematics. How have both research groups managed to devise highly effective interventions to improve math skills in early childhood?

Both groups believe that activities and materials should align with a learning goal, and they are guided by theory. As I already mentioned, Building Blocks is based on a theory of learning progressions (Clements & Sarama, 2008; Sarama, Clements, Starkey, Klein, & Wakeley, 2008). Siegler and Ramani's theory is called the cognitive alignment framework (Laski & Siegler, 2014; Siegler & Ramani, 2009).

The basic idea driving both theories is to be as specific as possible in defining the learning goal (for instance, spatial assembly skills) and to study exactly how it emerges in a learner (for example, the developmental progression of spatial assembly skills). Curriculum designers should be equally precise in designing a lesson or specific materials to promote that goal among learners at different points in the learning trajectory.

I suggest taking this approach one step further, by acknowledging the foundational cognitive skills at work when children use particular math skills. Looking at tasks through the lens of foundational skills may help teachers understand not just the type of mathematics task that they are teaching (such as subitizing or the number line), but also how the task makes demands on children's EF, motor, or spatial skills. That way, teachers can be more deliberate in providing children with opportunities to practice foundational skills along with the math-readiness skills.

Experts also note a potential role for computer and other digital tools in helping children understand particular concepts. They caution against old-fashioned manipulatives for their own sake, pointing out that if used poorly, manipulatives can be distracting. Furthermore, when designed and used well, computer representations of concepts may even be better than physical objects (Clements & McMillen, 1996).

SUMMARY

After children learn their memorizable "math facts," such as times tables, those rote tasks do not draw on EF to the degree that new and unfamiliar tasks do. But in early childhood, it is unrealistic to expect that most children will have automated any mathematics processes.

Based on this, it is not surprising that EF plays a big role in early mathematics knowledge and in children's readiness to learn math at school. The other two foundational cognitive skills—motor skills and spatial skills—also contribute meaningfully to math learning. Motor skills may lay a foundation for visuo-motor integration, which is a consistent predictor of mathematics achievement. Finally, spatial skills are intimately connected to certain math skills because of shared cognitive processes such as visualization and transformations that are involved in doing math problems that involve spatial concepts.

Understanding the foundational cognitive processes involved in mathematics can inform the development of successful activities and interventions, which include the Building Blocks curriculum and the Linear Number Board Game. The key to successful activity design, which is a recurring theme for virtually all the research I've reviewed, is to be thoughtful, intentional, and specific about how the learning activity or material supports particular skills. Intentional teacher guidance helps determine whether the activity offers children the desired opportunities to learn.

Board Games with Miriam

After learning about the many skills involved in early math, you decided to correct Miriam's counting errors during board games by encouraging her to point to each square and say a number word as she moves her game piece.

She was responsive to this, and so you decided to encourage all the children to be as precise as they can when they play games involving numbers, and you become more involved to guide them during play.

In carefully watching children play, you realized that before your "intervention," most children either had the aide count the spaces for them, or just quietly pretended that they knew how many squares to move and hoped no other children would notice. Miriam was the only child who counted loudly and incorrectly, which allowed you to notice her misconception. Luckily, gently guiding her to say one number word per space has the benefits of teaching the concept of one-to-one correspondence and fair game play to the entire class.

Part IV

GETTING THE MOST OUT OF PLAY

CHAPTER 9

Taking a Closer Look at Play

A small bell rings—it's free-choice time.

Nadia, who is 4, goes to a table in her preschool classroom where she sits down by herself. There's Play-Doh already at the table, and Nadia dumps it out and begins to smash it with the flat of her hand. She does this over and over again while she looks around the room, her attention wandering from area to area and then occasionally back to the flattening lump in front of her. After a while, she peels the disk of Play-Doh up from the table, reshapes it, and flattens it again with the same smashing hand motions.

Eli and Jean are playing shopkeeper. Eli stands behind a low wall made of milk crates; he is the clerk. Jean brings several items to Eli—a small wooden block, a paper clip, and a rubber chicken. "I want to buy these for my dinner," Jean says. Eli says, "Four dollars," and Jean pretends to open an imaginary purse. She hands Eli a pretend credit card. "Thank you for your business," Eli says. "You have a nice day."

Marcus sits down at a table where his classroom's aide takes the top off a plastic container with hundreds of small, plastic "beads" that look like tiny colored toilet paper rolls, called Perler beads. These beads can be placed on a white pegboard, which comes in different shapes, and then ironed so the beads melt together. Marcus chooses a picture with the design of a spaceship, and decides on a square-shaped pegboard like the one in the picture. The classroom aide says to the children working at the table, "Think about where to begin your design; I suggest the middle." Marcus carefully picks his first bead, a red one, from the plastic container and places it in the center of the pegboard.

Each of the above examples could happen during "free play" or "free-choice time" in a U.S. preschool classroom. If you were a researcher or school administrator who entered the classroom to observe and create categories based on children's activities, you might consider the activities of Nadia, Eli and Jean, and Marcus very much the same.

In all three scenarios, children make a choice about their activity, without adult input into what they "should" be doing, and physical materials are involved in their play. But there are some key differences in these children's activities as well:

- Nadia is not interacting with anyone else, and her interactions with the Play-Doh are simplistic and repetitive. This activity is not difficult enough to keep her attention, which wanders around the classroom even as she sits quietly at her chosen spot. Even if the activity is too easy for her, the adults in the room appreciate when children work quietly on their own.
- In contrast, Eli and Jean have entered a world of their own where they turn real and pretend materials into something else using their imaginations. These two create their own rules for play based on the roles they have taken on, and they are engaged in what many people, especially early childhood teachers, probably think of as stereotypically "good" play.
- Marcus works largely by himself, though with an adult nearby and on a project that was initially guided—that is, planned and facilitated—by the adult. He must concentrate to work with the small, tube-like Perler beads. Instead of inventing his own design, he is copying an existing model. This may cause discomfort in some teachers, who might propose that Marcus should be allowed to exercise creativity and choose what to do with the beads instead of copying what someone else made.

This chapter examines the complex concept of play in early childhood settings. Play is considered an essential learning experience for young children. Though the concept of free play in particular enjoys a great deal of support from a diverse set of research-based and theoretical writings, much of the research that is used to support free play has tended to involve children playing outside of early school settings or does not look at classroom play directly. This mismatch introduces two questions, of *how much* and *what types of play* should prevail in actual early childhood classrooms.

To address these questions, I report results from a large national study of a diverse group of preschoolers' experiences with unstructured free play compared with a variety of other activities (Chien et al., 2010). Generalizations about the universal benefits of free play appear unwarranted when looking at this robust observational data from hundreds of classrooms. The take-home message is that children who spent the *most* time in unstructured free play actually learned *less* in the majority of skills assessed.

Because these findings may seem counterintuitive given the large amount of literature that is pro-play, I go into them in some detail to answer the question: What, if anything, should replace unstructured free play?

I suggest a way to improve children's foundational skills through another type of play called *guided object play*. To close the chapter, I explore a study of the Minds in Motion after-school curriculum, which improved 5- and 6-year-olds' foundational cognitive skills through guided object play.

> *THEME:* Play is fun, motivating, and child directed. In classroom observations of actual early environments, all children do not freely play in ways that are associated with learning, however. Instead, adult-guided opportunities to interact with objects (*guided object play*) invites children to exercise their EF, motor, and spatial skills in developmentally appropriate activities.

UNDERSTANDING PLAY

According to experts, many activities can be considered play, but playful activity has some key elements (Burghardt, 2012; Weisberg, Hirsh-Pasek, & Golinkoff, 2013). Consistent with scholarly definitions, in a study for the Minnesota Children's Museum, Rachel White (2013) defined play as having at least one of the following elements, where activities with more of the elements are considered more playful than activities with fewer:

- ***Fun***
- Done for its own sake
- Process-oriented (that is, the end product is not important)
- ***Freely chosen*** (that is, ***child-directed***)
- ***Actively engaging***
- Nonliteral, or having imaginary elements

White (2013) notes that the elements in bold in the above list are required for an activity to be considered play. "Fun" activities are motivating and enjoyable. "Freely chosen" activities mean the child exercises choice and freedom in deciding what to pursue and how to direct the activity, giving rise to the term *child directed*. And "actively engaging" contrasts with passive engagement like watching or listening. Active engagement suggests that the child engages in physical movements and mental effort that is still enjoyable.

Given these defining elements of play, White (2013) further described five types of playful activity, based on the focus of the activity: social, object, pretend, physical, and media. The categories are not mutually exclusive—for example, creating a video with a friend would combine social and media play. In addition, each of these types can vary on a continuum from unstructured, fully child-directed play to adult-guided activities.

Because experts do not consider activities that are *entirely* structured by adults to be play, the term *guided play* refers to adult involvement to facilitate learning that is still child-centered (White, 2013). That is, the child exercises substantial choice in selecting and pursuing the activity.

The Child-Directed Versus Teacher-Directed Distinction

The degree of choice in the activity introduces a distinction between child-directed activity contrasted with teacher-directed activity. These fall on two ends of a continuum. On one end is completely child-directed activity, with no adult involvement other than to keep children safe. The child selects where to play, with what materials and with which social partners to play, and for how long to play.

On the other end of the continuum is completely teacher-directed activity, where the adult makes all these decisions: The teacher tells the child where to play, how to play, and with whom to play and determines the length of the play session. Teacher-directed activity is also called *didactic*.

At different places in the middle of the continuum are activities that balance the extent to which they are child-directed versus teacher-directed. Table 9.1 shows examples of five types of play, depending on whether it is free or guided, with some of the children from the vignette opening this chapter. For contrast, examples of teacher-centered didactic activities are shown in the far-right column.

Early childhood educators tend to endorse the child-directed end of the continuum. Textbooks and curriculum materials, as well as the representative texts of organizations like the National Association for the Education of Young Children (NAEYC; Bredekamp & Copple, 2009), propose that children must be able to freely explore and learn from the world around them. Survey data show that early childhood professionals in the United States believe in the merits of unstructured free play in particular, which falls at the "completely child-directed" end of the continuum (the far left column in Table 9.1).

Specifically, a group of professors and teachers of early childhood reported that based on their expertise, unstructured activities are more beneficial for young children's learning than adult-structured activities such as book reading or a trip to the zoo (Fisher, Hirsh-Pasek, Golinkoff, & Gryfe, 2008). Interestingly, compared to early childhood professors and teachers, U.S. mothers endorsed a wider variety of activities as play, including those activities structured by an adult.

Finally, a substantial body of research informs the philosophy that play is learning (Fisher et al., 2008; White, 2013), with scholars from disciplines including medicine and psychology noting the potential health and cognitive benefits of unstructured play in children of all ages (Burdette & Whitaker, 2005; Sattelmair & Ratey, 2009).

Table 9.1. Five Types of Free Play and Guided Play Contrasted with Didactic Practice

Type of Play	Free	Guided	Didactic
Object	Nadia (from the vignette at the beginning of this chapter) smashes Play-Doh.	The teacher offers Nadia several ideas for what she could build with the Play-Doh, and Nadia chooses one.	The teacher tells children to make a snowman with their Play-Doh.
Social	A toddler teases another child to "chase me, chase me!"	Parent initiates game of peek-a-boo with her infant, then follows her baby's lead.	Teacher directs her 1st-graders in a game of Telephone.
Pretend	Eli and Jean decide to play "grocery store" and choose materials and a space in which to play.	The teacher helps Eli and Jean choose grocery store roles, and reminds them of actions their characters might take.	The teacher chooses a story for Drama Time, assigns roles to each child, and coaches them in acting it out.
Physical	On the playground, Marcus and Jack engage in rough-and-tumble play.	The teacher helps Jack lead a game of Red Light, Green Light with his peers.	The teacher explains that Friday is Kickball Day and tells children the rules.
Media	Grace, a 2nd-grader, uses a tablet-based app to make a short film about her cousin.	Mrs. Lowden helps her kindergarten class take digital pictures of a field trip, and then write their own stories to go with the photos.	A teacher tells the class they will be making a movie about the school garden, and assigns tasks to each child.

Constructivism and Play

The play-is-learning philosophy has origins in a learning theory called *constructivism*. Though I won't be able to do this subject justice here, I highlight the relevant features for this chapter, and suggest further readings (e.g., Fosnot, 2005).

Constructivism is the idea that rather than being empty containers that adults fill with information, children are active learners. That is, they *construct* new information by applying a combination of what they already know with what the situation *affords*, or offers (Piaget, 1963; see also Chapters 2 and 4 for more on affordances).

Piaget emphasized children's *independent discovery* leading to new knowledge (informing the development of discovery learning approaches—see, for example, Alfieri, Brooks, Aldrich, & Tenenbaum, 2011). Another key feature of constructivism is that it occurs within a *social community* under the guidance of a more able other (Vygotsky, 1978). Vygotsky wrote that *"human learning presupposes a specific social nature and a process by which children grow into the intellectual life around them"* (p. 88, emphasis in original).

Combining the discovery and social features of constructivism in the preschool classroom positions the teacher's role as a guide or facilitator of children's self-directed learning. Given a safe situation rich with learning possibilities, the child's interests and motivation should ideally inform the direction and nature of their activities; hence, the term *child-centered* practice.

A teacher or other adult who uses *teacher-directed* methods controls a situation by telling children what to learn or what to do next. Children in teacher-directed settings are thought to become discouraged or disengaged because their own interests are not respected and thereby learn less than children who are left alone to explore a safe and enriching environment. Supporting this idea, a widely reported experiment involving 85 mostly White, mid-SES preschoolers tested in a science museum showed that children discovered more creative uses for a novel toy when they were allowed to freely explore it, compared to those who were told precisely what the toy did (Bonawitz et al., 2011).

Another study of actual early childhood classrooms showed negative effects when teachers used didactic practices. This particular study included 227 preschoolers and kindergartners from low- and mid-SES backgrounds. Didactic practice constituted direct instruction in whole-group settings—in other words, teachers telling children what to do most of the time (Stipek, Feiler, Daniels, & Milburn, 1995).

Outcomes of children in didactic settings were compared with outcomes for children in classrooms with more child-centered practices where children were allowed choice and freedom and the option of working in small groups. In didactic settings, children learned more in reading, but learned less in math and were less motivated than those in the child-centered classrooms. In other words, children in the early childhood programs where they are offered choice had better attitudes toward school than children in programs where they were told what to do (Stipek et al., 1995).

Child-Directed Practices Are Associated with Positive Outcomes

Aligned with the findings by Stipek at al. (1995), there are many studies of people of all ages that show that having control in one's choices is crucial for maintaining interest and engagement, which is also good for learning (Deci

& Ryan, 2000). This favorable evidence for control and choice is prominent in studies of motivation, but also appears in studies of educators' teaching beliefs as indicators of high-quality teaching practices (Pianta et al., 2005) and research on effective parenting (Grolnick & Farkas, 2002).

Evidence in favor of child-directed parenting. Research studies on parenting, along with many popular parenting magazines and websites, reiterate the importance of offering children choice, especially with regard to managing their behavior. Grolnick and Ryan (1989) documented that 66 middle-SES elementary-school-age children whose parents involved them in making decisions and who supported their children's independence were better able to manage their behavior in school, got better grades, and were seen as better adjusted by their teachers, compared to children whose parents reported more controlling parenting behaviors.

Still other studies indicate that when parents allow their young children to voice their preferences, help children understand the reasoning behind a request, and avoid physical punishment, children are less likely to violently act out (Choe, Olson, & Sameroff, 2013).

Evidence in favor of child-directed teaching. Among early childhood professionals, teachers with child-centered beliefs tend to provide generally higher-quality learning environments. This means engaging in more responsive, warm, and organized interactions with children, compared with teachers who have adult-centered beliefs (Pianta et al., 2005).

A teacher with child-centered beliefs would agree with a statement such as "Children should be allowed to disagree with their parents if they feel their own ideas are better," whereas a teacher with adult-centered beliefs would agree with the statement "Children should always obey the teacher" (Pianta et al., 2005, p. 151).

In turn, compared to teachers with adult-centered beliefs, preschool teachers with child-centered beliefs tend to offer more cognitively challenging learning activities to children, and their classrooms spend less time in large-group settings—considered developmentally inappropriate. There is growing concern about the highly structured, academic focus of the typical kindergarten setting in the United States, driven by accountability and testing policies to increase achievement scores (Bassok, Latham, & Rorem, 2016; Weisberg et al., 2013).

RESULTS FROM A STUDY IN 701 PRESCHOOL CLASSROOMS

Based on results from parenting and child- versus teacher-directed teaching, the case for play seems strong. But, as with most concepts in this book, simple definitions and conclusions can hide nuances that turn out to be important for understanding how to foster young children's development in specific skill domains. For example, when play is translated into early childhood practice, empirical research suggests that something important is missing.

When Nina Chien was a postdoctoral fellow at the University of California, San Diego, she and her colleagues examined observational data collected for a large study of preschool classrooms conducted by the National Center for Early Development and Learning (NCEDL; Early et al., 2005), funded by the U.S. Department of Education. Using this large data set, Chien and her colleagues (2010) were able to look at how 2,751 children—average age 4 years, 7 months—spent their time in more than 700 classrooms across 10 U.S. states.

From a larger group of children with permission to participate in the study, the NCEDL observers watched four randomly selected children in each classroom over 2 days, spending 2.5 hours in the classroom each day.

Given the flexible schedule and activities of the typical preschool classroom, the observers coded what each of the four individual children was doing every 5 minutes. Then they analyzed the observations to see whether there were any patterns. Specifically, the researchers wondered whether, even though 2,751 children likely engaged in 2,751 different combinations of activities, it was possible to describe how they spent their time with a small number of general themes.

How Preschoolers Spend the Day: Too Much Unstructured Time?

The researchers identified four different groups of children. Within a particular group—called *profiles*—children spent their time in similar activities but differed in the amount of time they spent in each activity. Important to note, these four profiles were not equally distributed with 25% of children in each profile. Instead, over half (51%) of the children fell into the first pattern, Profile 1.

Based on what you know of the popularity of unstructured free play, what activity do you think distinguished Profile 1? If your guess had something to do with free play, you were right: The researchers called this profile with the most children the "Free Play" group, because these children spent about 41% of their time, or about 1 hour of the 2.5-hour day, in *unstructured free play* (called free-choice) activities. These activities were defined as "Child selects what and where to play or learn, engaging in activities such as individual art projects, blocks, pretend play, and reading" (Chien et al., 2010, p. 1538). The second most common activity these children did, *gross motor activities*, took up about 12 minutes (8%).

In contrast, only 9% of the children fell into Profile 2, called the "Individual Instruction" profile. The activity that best defined this profile, and took up just over half an hour (21%) of children's time, was called *individual activity* where they worked by themselves.

What's the difference between *free play* and *individual activity*? In free play, children chose for themselves where and with whom to spend their time, whereas in individual activity, children "each work on a project independently, such as a worksheet or on the computer. The teacher moves around to help" (Chien et al., 2010, p. 1538). In other words, individual activities were carried out by children but were selected and guided by the teacher. In the study I mentioned earlier that found differences in mothers' and early childhood teachers' views of play, mothers would most likely have counted such individual activities as play, but teachers would not (Fisher et al., 2008).

Children in Profile 2 also spent the relative most time, 26 minutes (17%), in a separate category: *fine motor activities* such as "stringing beads, building with Legos, cutting, or using crayons and markers" (p. 1538). By some definitions, working independently on fine motor activities could still be considered in the broader category of play, but may not be free-choice activities. Referring to Table 9.1, fine motor activities also fall into the category of "object play" because they involve physical materials, versus social or pretend play.

Just over one-quarter (27%) of all the children observed fell into Profile 3, which the researchers called the "Group Instruction" profile. This was because their most common activity was as a whole group, taking up about 54 minutes (36%) of their time; they also spent much more time than children in the other groups in small-group activity, which took up 17 minutes (11%) of their time.

Finally, the last profile—Profile 4—represented just 13% of the children. Like Profile 1, these children's most common activity was free play, with about 44 minutes spent (29%). But what really distinguished Profile 4 was their time with the teacher: On average, Profile 4 got a whopping 32 minutes (21%) of one-on-one time, and 9 minutes of special responses (6%) with the teacher. This was more than twice the one-on-one time with an adult of any other group. So this group was called the "Scaffolded Learning" profile.

Scaffolding is another common early childhood term that means an adult helps children accomplish an activity they could otherwise not carry out on their own—just as a scaffold allows builders to make progress on a building that they couldn't otherwise complete (Wood, Bruner, & Ross, 1976). Scaffolding counts as *guided play* (Weisberg et al., 2013), with examples in Table 9.1 and described in more detail later.

Preschool Activities Connected to Learning Outcomes

The results about the four groups in Chien et al.'s (2010) study show the types of activities that real children tend to engage in when they are in actual preschool classrooms. A follow-up analysis performed as part of the same research article helps address the question of whether a particular profile of play is connected with learning outcomes. In other words, what if one of the four ways of spending time appears to be better for children—in terms of their development in academic and cognitive skills?

There were three clear findings in terms of the amount that children in the different profiles learned over the preschool year:

1. Children in the "Free Play" profile learned *less* than children in the other groups on the following specific skills: naming letters, letter-word identification, teachers' reports of children's language and literacy skills, number counting, and writing their names.

    This doesn't appear to be because of the characteristics of children in the "Free Play" profile being different from children in the other profiles. Even looking only within the "Free Play" profile, children from low-SES backgrounds learned *less* compared to those from more advantaged backgrounds. This means that children of low-SES whose pattern of activities placed them into the "Free Play" profile were at a double disadvantage because they were already in the profile that learned the least overall.

2. Children in the "Scaffolded Learning" profile learned as much as children in the "Individual Instruction" and "Group Instruction" profiles in letter naming, letter-word identification, teacher-reported literacy, naming numbers, and numbers counted.

    This is important because children in the "Scaffolded Learning" profile also spent substantial amounts of time in free play. But they spent more than twice as much time individually interacting with their teachers as children in the "Free Play" profile.

3. Children in the "Individual Instruction" profile—who spent the relatively largest amounts of their time in individual and fine motor activities—learned the *most* on applied problems, a mathematics assessment requiring a range of quantitative knowledge and skills.

    In addition, within the "Individual Instruction" profile, children of low SES learned *more* compared to more advantaged children on letter-word identification, numbers counted, and early mathematics.

In conclusion, this study of more than 2,700 children in 701 preschool classrooms doesn't favor large amounts of unstructured free play, defined as open-ended activity that children select themselves. The study does, however, suggest that a *combination* of unstructured free play, adult-guided activity, and individual and fine motor activities are associated with children learning relatively more in multiple domains.

FINDING A MIDDLE GROUND IN GUIDED OBJECT PLAY

For the remainder of this book, I devote special attention to a specific type of guided play that can provide those constraints necessary for children to learn foundational cognitive skills:

> *Guided object play* combines guided play with object play. In the example from the first row, middle column of Table 9.1, the teacher helps Nadia choose something she could make with the Play-Doh. Another example from this chapter's opening scene is with Marcus, who is being helped by the classroom aide to copy a spaceship design using Perler beads.

In guided object play, adults help focus children's attention on play with objects and encourage specific actions with those objects. Not coincidentally, several of the interventions reviewed in this book engage children in guided object play, with potential benefits for EF, motor skills, and spatial skills.

Bonawitz et al. (2011) note a trade-off inherent in such encouragement, because of their study showing that when adults specify how materials should be used, children explore them less. At the same time, there are possible benefits when adults provide clear guidance to children about how to use materials. These benefits should be weighed against the likelihood of learning occurring without such intervention.

In their words, "The costs and benefits of instruction depend on how knowledgeable and helpful the teacher is, and on how likely the learner is to discover either the target information or novel information on [their] own" (Bonawitz et al., 2011, p. 328).

Another way to think about this is, if adults get overly involved in the play, children may not discover on their own, but if adults don't get involved enough, children may not learn on their own.

Finding the right amount of adult involvement is a puzzle that teachers need to solve for each individual child. I propose that when children's EF, motor, or spatial skills are underdeveloped, guided object play is appropriate. Next, let's look in depth at the evolution of a successful intervention based on guided object play: an after-school curriculum called Minds in Motion.

MINDS IN MOTION: A GUIDED OBJECT PLAY CURRICULUM THAT IMPROVES LOW-INCOME CHILDREN'S EF AND SPATIAL SKILLS

Minds in Motion is a 5-month after-school curriculum that was created at the University of Virginia when I worked as a research scientist there. The curriculum evolved after research professor David Grissmer noticed that children who started kindergarten with strong fine motor skills had higher reading and math achievement later in elementary school, even after accounting for their earlier achievement (Grissmer et al., 2010). Similar patterns emerged across three large data sets, including a sample of 20,000 children that was nationally representative for U.S. entering kindergartners in 1998–1999.

When I joined the research team, we worked to understand these results more fully, asking: Why are fine motor skills such an impressive and robust predictor of later achievement?

We discovered that it was children's *visuo-motor integration*, measured with copying tasks like the Beery VMI (see also Chapter 5), not their other fine motor skills, that contributed so strongly to their achievement (Cameron, Brock, et al., 2012). Other researchers have since replicated this finding as well (Carlson et al., 2013). The pattern alerted us to what clinical psychologists have known for years: Visuo-motor integration is a highly complex spatial skill and is a common element of IQ tests by major publishers.

Still, the studies that pointed to visuo-motor integration as a key ingredient in children's school readiness were all correlational. There was no way to know for sure whether improving children's visuo-motor integration would help their school readiness. Maybe children with strong visuo-motor integration were good at other things that were actually responsible for school readiness.

To sort this out, Grissmer and another researcher, Andrew Mashburn (now of Portland State University), sought to test the hypothesis that engaging children in copying designs would improve their cognitive and academic skills. To make sure that no other factors could explain possible results in favor of the activities, Grissmer and Mashburn used a school-based experimental design, known as a randomized control trial (RCT).

First, they hired two people with curriculum design experience. Keeping in mind the importance of visuo-motor integration (a constructional task that requires spatial skills), former special educator Beth Cottone and then–doctoral student Wei-Bing Chen got to work. They created a multiweek curriculum designed for after-school delivery called Minds in Motion. Then, the research team developed the intervention, tested first with a diverse group of mostly mid-SES children in the mid-Atlantic region, and then with mostly African American children from high-poverty communities in the South (for details on these two samples, see Kim et al., 2017). Clinical school psychologist Julia Blodgett designed the assessment plan for both sites.

Laura Brock of the College of Charleston led the work in South Carolina (Brock, Murrah, Cottone, Mashburn, & Grissmer, in press). In her study, 87 kindergarten and 1st-grade children were randomly assigned to either treatment ($n = 44$) or control ($n = 43$) groups. All children were recruited from an after-school program that ran a social-emotional learning curriculum for 3 hours per day, 5 days per week. Children in the control group engaged in the activities that were part of that curriculum, which ranged from small- to large-group games and playful activities designed to help children understand, manage, and respond appropriately to their own and others' feelings.

As part of their time in the after-school program, children in the Minds in Motion treatment group attended small groups of four to seven children that met for 45 minutes per day, four times per week. Minds in Motion intervention leaders were after-school program staff who received 11 hours of additional training, including training in how to individualize the curriculum activities to the child's skill level—similar to scaffolding.

Activities varied, but emphasized constructional tasks using commercially available building toys. More details about the curriculum materials and activities are reported in Brock et al. (in press), but the main idea was for adults to engage children in guided object play with the materials.

For most constructional tasks, Minds in Motion leaders showed children a model or a picture of a model, and also showed them how to make one "just like it." Materials included a range of arts and crafts materials and manipulatives such as wooden blocks, colored vinyl shapes, heat-fused beads, and stained glass; and various materials such as yarn, popsicle sticks, and cardboard tubes used to make projects such as God's eyes and homemade musical instruments.

Often, children got to choose from among different models before beginning, and they were allowed time to freely play and explore the materials after completing the constructional task. Additional brief but regularly used activities also included worksheets focusing on motor precision and visuo-motor coordination, as well as group activities where children practiced EF skills such as waiting and taking turns through games like Simon Says.

The results, analyzed by Hank Murrah (now of Auburn University), were quite striking. Children in Minds in Motion improved on a nationally norm-referenced assessment from around the bottom third of scores to the middle group of scores. Results were strongest for EF, but were also impressive for spatial skills. Analyses were complex, but the power of the intervention is easy to illustrate with simple mean differences: Children in the control group improved an average of 8.82 and 0.84 points in EF and spatial skills, respectively. In contrast, children in Minds in Motion improved an average of 19.15 and 7.59 points in EF and spatial skills, respectively. Figure 9.1 displays these differences for each group.

The final important result was that children's regular classroom teachers, who had no knowledge of whether children were participating in Minds in Motion or the control group, noticed differences in children's behavior. Specifically, using rating scales, teachers reported that children who attended Minds in Motion had better self-control and fewer behavioral problems, compared to children in the control group (Brock et al., in press).

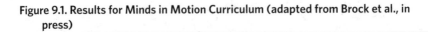

Figure 9.1. Results for Minds in Motion Curriculum (adapted from Brock et al., in press)

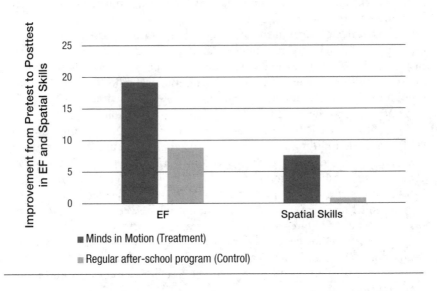

Although it's a small study, and therefore needs to be replicated, the success of Minds in Motion corroborates the review of studies by Uttal et al. (2013): It's possible to improve children's spatial skills with specifically designed activities, where children (1) practice cognitive processes, such as perceptual judgments and comparisons and transformations, and (2) perform constructional tasks using their bodies and engaging, age-appropriate materials. That Minds in Motion also improved children's EF and classroom behavior suggests that spatial skills are interwoven with other aspects of school readiness and academic skills. Results even suggest the intriguing idea that improving children's spatial skills might foster their learning and behavior in other areas.

SUMMARY

Play is fun, child-directed, and active. Playful activity can vary along a continuum from child-directed to adult-guided, and results from many studies on parenting and education bolster the importance of children having meaningful choice in their activities. Most research has not, however, examined the activities in which children in actual early childhood classrooms engage.

One large-scale, national study indicates that many preschool classrooms provide too much unstructured free play without enough adult guidance. And large amounts of unstructured free play are associated with children learning less compared with children who engaged in a combination of unstructured free play, adult-guided activity, and individual fine motor activities. This research suggests that teachers should get more involved in children's play than is typical in unstructured free play.

Minds in Motion is one exciting program based on guided object play that improves children's EF, spatial skills, and classroom behavior over the transition to formal schooling. Guided object play is developmentally appropriate because it is still child-centered but involves adult-child interactions and individualized support that many children need. I expand the idea that guided object play can help children learn foundational cognitive skills in Chapter 10.

Guided Object Play with Nadia

After learning about the benefits of guided object play, and the drawbacks of children having too much time to themselves in preschool, you decide to join Nadia the next time she chooses to work with Play-Doh. You show her some images of Play-Doh animals you found on the Internet, and ask if she likes any of the animals she sees. She chooses a kitten and asks for your help to make one like it. You show her how to roll the dough into different-size balls and then make the tiny ears pointy on one end. After she makes the kitten, you encourage her to make a toy for the kitten to play with . . . but you leave it to her to decide what to make. Nadia is receptive to this small amount of guidance, and she is able to do much more with the Play-Doh after your session with her.

CHAPTER 10

Using Guided Object Play to Explicitly Teach the Foundational Cognitive Skills

My main goal so far has been to show how three foundational cognitive skills (EF, motor, and spatial skills) support children's learning across school-readiness domains. In this concluding chapter, I argue for continued emphases on nonacademic as well as early academic experiences in preschool, with special attention to the nature and quality of those experiences. I explain why an explicit focus on these three foundational cognitive skills in early childhood classrooms is appropriate for many children.

I believe early childhood teachers should strive to spend more of their time in high-quality interactions with individual and small groups of children playing with materials in activities and games. In other words, I propose that early childhood professionals integrate more *guided object play* into their classrooms. This proposal is consistent with policy and research-supported positions on developmentally appropriate practice in early childhood (Administration on Children Youth and Families/Head Start Bureau, 2015; Weisberg et al., 2013).

Making more time for guided object play can't happen without changing the context in which teachers teach and children learn. Changes are needed at multiple levels of the systems that support early childhood development and education. As a society and in our individual communities, we must invest in the training, compensation, and cultural valuing of the professionals who devote their lives to careers in early childhood education.

> **CONCLUDING THEME:** Taking a little more time for guided object play with children is a developmentally appropriate way for early childhood professionals to explicitly target EF, motor skills, and spatial skills. For teachers to be able to engage in adequate amounts of guided object play with children, our government officials and community leaders must do a better job of investing in early childhood education and research to improve its quality.

GUIDED OBJECT PLAY CAN ADDRESS LEARNING OPPORTUNITY GAPS

In Chapter 2, I discussed income and education inequality. Yet I also pointed out that SES inequality is really just a proxy for unequal learning resources and opportunities—a concept known as the *opportunity gap.*

Compared with mid- and upper-SES communities, early home environments in low-SES communities are less likely to offer children learning experiences, opportunities, and interactions that are associated with school readiness. These differences in early learning resources and opportunities contribute to children demonstrating very different skill levels when it's time to go to school. But preschool and early elementary school can supplement certain learning opportunities that many families living in low-SES conditions don't provide to their children because of lack of money, education, or time. The key is finding the right activities, those that will help close the opportunity gap.

I want to be clear about something really important: The opportunity gap that children from low-SES backgrounds experience is not a lack of didactic, teacher-controlled experiences. Instead, evidence points to a gap in individualized interactions around play-based materials and activities, which mid- and upper-SES families are more likely to provide to their children than are low-SES families (Potter et al., 2012). Didactic, teacher-directed approaches are actually associated with negative consequences for motivation and certain measures of achievement among children from all SES backgrounds (Stipek et al., 1995).

Closing the opportunity gap in adult guidance in child-centered play situations at preschool could be especially helpful for children from low-SES backgrounds. Relatively more teacher guidance is also consistent with a review of 164 studies that found that *guided discovery* rather than entirely unassisted discovery learning resulted in the most learning (Alfieri et al., 2011). Unfortunately, the observational study of 701 preschool classrooms that I described in Chapter 9 shows that the children most likely to engage in scaffolded activities (which align best with my definition of guided play) are those from mid- and upper-SES backgrounds (Chien et al., 2010). Children from low-SES backgrounds spend relatively more time in individual instruction settings, which offer the potential for teacher guidance but are less playful according to the definition of play.

Combining the fun, active, and child-directed aspects of play with gently guided experiences that allow youngsters to develop their foundational cognitive skills may be an essential element of efforts to foster school readiness among all children, but especially those from low-SES backgrounds. Such an approach echoes advice from Temple University professors Deena Skolnick Weisberg and Kathy Hirsh-Pasek and University of Delaware professor Roberta Michnick Golinkoff (Weisberg et al., 2013). They argue that *guided play* is a developmentally appropriate middle ground that sits between free play to one extreme and direct, didactic instruction to the other.

Guided play is also consistent with Vygotsky's (1978) seminal writings about social constructivism requiring the involvement of a more able other in the learning process, as well as with the more recent evolutions of his ideas (Bodrova & Leong, 2006). Weisberg et al. (2013) define *guided play* as

> a metaphor for any type of learning that encourages a learner to be an active and engaged partner in the learning process and that *provides a constrained way for helping children focus* on the outcomes of interest. (p. 109, italics added)

Guided object play remains child-directed in many ways. Crucially, adults can help children focus their attention on the materials and features of materials that will best exercise their developing executive function, motor, and spatial skills.

TEACHERS ENACT THE CURRICULUM
THROUGH THEIR INTERACTIONS WITH CHILDREN

There is strong recent evidence that specially designed preschool and early elementary activities can bolster children's language, emergent literacy, and mathematics skills as stand-alone lessons or interventions (Ramani et al., 2012; Wasik, Hindman, & Snell, 2016), or as part of the regular curriculum (Connor et al., 2010; Justice, Mashburn, Pence, & Wiggins, 2008; Sarama, Lange, Clements, & Wolfe, 2012). Based on the research I've reviewed in this book that EF, motor skills, and spatial skills also respond to intervention, foundational cognitive skills should be added to the list of skills that early childhood classrooms support through curriculum shifts and individualized guided activities.

Changing curricula and activities to focus on foundational cognitive skills is only a first step, however: Early childhood teachers are the ones who actually enact the curricula, and teacher behaviors matter at least as much as the curriculum in relation to children's learning. Efforts to enact new programs indicate that it may be especially challenging for teachers to find the "magic middle" of guided play.

For example, the Tools of the Mind preschool curriculum was designed to help teachers explicitly teach EF and self-regulation to their young children (Bodrova & Leong, 2007). Unfortunately, a large-scale evaluation showed that this curriculum (Farran, Wilson, Meador, Norvell, & Nesbitt, 2015) did not realize the promise of early work (Barnett et al., 2008).

Observational data suggest that null and negative results for the Tools of the Mind condition emerged because the curriculum didn't change the right things in the classroom. On the one hand, children in classrooms whose teachers who were trained to use the curriculum increased their amounts of time in pretend play (which was more common in Tools classrooms than in control classrooms). But on the other, teachers' general social and language interactions and children's learning behaviors were largely the same in both types of classrooms, whether Tools or control.

What's more, in some Tools classrooms, pretend playtime became a *teacher-directed activity*! How can this be?

The evaluators speculate that from their training in the Tools curriculum, teachers took away the idea that children needed to spend a certain amount of time in pretend play. When teachers noticed children failing to spend adequate amounts of time in pretend play, they got more heavily involved in the play themselves. But too many teacher reminders during pretend play could turn it into a didactic activity, which runs counter to the philosophy of children practicing EF on their own, which is the basis for Tools of the Mind (Bodrova & Leong, 2007).

This example contains a lesson for thinking about how to support children's foundational cognitive skills through guided object play. Hugely important is the teachers' understanding of the purpose of an activity and the interactions that are needed to help children get the most from it. And to get the most from it, researchers must help teachers identify the specific, classroom-contextualized behaviors that children should demonstrate in a given activity (Whitehurst, 2016).

I believe one reason it's so difficult to teach the foundational cognitive skills is because in most curricula, these skills are "hidden" in that they are not usually explicitly assessed, nor are they direct targets of instruction. In Chapter 6, I described research that connects the foundational skills with approaches to learning in the classroom. Based on this, children with underdeveloped foundational skills may appear bored or disinterested, or they may even act out because they lack the EF, motor, or spatial skills to effectively engage in an activity. But sometimes even when children's behavior appears appropriate for the learning situation, their behaviors may signal that they need some additional help.

For example, Michael and Miriam like to spend time in the classroom's reading nook. Miriam usually suggests that they take all the books off the shelf and stack them on top of one another. As long as they don't disrupt the classroom, the teacher decides that the pair are having fun with books and learning to enjoy them as objects first. She assumes they will eventually begin to look at the pages "when they are ready."

Looking through the lens of foundational cognitive skills, children stacking books might be ready for additional guidance. For example, the teacher could assist children in practicing the fine motor skills of opening books properly and turning the pages gently. Compared to leaving children to play on their own with the books, this type of guidance for the foundational motor skills specific to book reading would gently support children's emerging awareness of print.

MAKING TIME FOR GUIDED OBJECT PLAY

High-quality learning opportunities in the early childhood environment arise from three types of resources: appropriate use of learning materials, positive teacher–child interactions based on positive relationships, and time (Hamre, Hatfield, Pianta, & Jamil, 2013). If one of these is missing, the learning opportunity will be less successful.

Learning materials should be thoughtfully chosen and based on theory and practice. If a caregiver is not able to spend time interacting with a child, the best materials will just sit on a shelf or will be used for purposes that might be fun but may not foster foundational skills, as in the reading nook example above.

As another example, two out of the three resources exist in a home with a good parent–child relationship and a parent who spends time with a child. But if there are no books or appropriate toys in the home, the child would have no opportunity to learn what the materials might have made possible or what other children learn when they do have all three resources.

Finally, children must spend regular amounts of time on deliberate activities where they can practice their skills to achieve automaticity and fluency. I mentioned the idea of dose in Chapters 3 and 4. In the next section, I explain that for guided object play to work its magic, materials must be used effectively in the context of positive child–teacher relationships.

Relationships: Guided Object Play Incorporates Teacher Scaffolding

Researchers at the University of Virginia Center for Advanced Study for Teaching and Learning (CASTL) have led a great deal of research showing that supportive, responsive, and positive adult involvement is related to children learning more and exhibiting more adaptive classroom behaviors (Hamre & Pianta, 2001; Merritt, Wanless, Rimm-Kaufman, Cameron, & Peugh, 2012).

What's more, the success of learning materials and activities depends largely on the interactions that children have with their caregivers and teachers in both preschool (Mashburn et al., 2008) and elementary school (Cameron Ponitz, Rimm-Kaufman, Grimm, & Curby, 2009). High-quality interactions can even help close the opportunity gap by providing children with guided interactions that can compensate for risk factors such as low SES or behavior problems (Hamre & Pianta, 2005).

So, ideally, learning experiences to support foundational cognitive skills would occur in the context of warm and nurturing relationships where children are challenged and encouraged in those challenges. Without caregivers whom children trust and with whom children are comfortable learning, the learning activities are unlikely to matter (Curby et al., 2013).

In addition, because EF and self-regulation are still developing in the early childhood period, many children need help from their teachers with their attention, impulses, and choices. One CASTL study used an idea called Banking Time, where preschool teachers "bank" time with the two or three children with whom they have the most difficulty in the classroom (Williford et al., 2016). This study asked teachers to spend 20–30 minutes per week with these individual children, with the fairly simple goal of creating a space for positive interactions and relationship building.

Results were positive and showed that spending special, "set-aside" time either on activities of the child's choice or something that the teacher decided to work on with the child resulted in less problem behavior, compared to a control group of children who didn't receive extra time with their teacher.

Remember the positive results for the "Scaffolded Learning" profile of children in Chapter 9? Those children spent more than twice as much time individually interacting with their teachers as children in the "Free Play" profile, and they also learned more (Chien et al., 2010). Together, these studies reveal positive associations with children's social and academic development, with more quality time spent interacting with teachers.

As part of a comprehensive curriculum, guided object play offers one context for the teacher and child or a small group of children to engage in a fun activity together where their attention is directed to materials that the children can see and touch. Guided object play introduces children to toys and learning materials that they are likely to find novel and engaging, and supports children in using the materials in ways that exercise their EF, motor skills, and spatial skills (Brock et al., in press). Such play corresponds with points made by Weisberg et al. (2013):

> In guided play, adults initiate the learning process, constrain the learning goals, and are responsible for maintaining focus on these goals even as the child guides his or her own discovery. In guided play, teachers might enhance children's exploration and learning by commenting on their discoveries, co-playing along with the children, asking open-ended questions about what children are finding, or exploring the materials in ways that children might not have thought to do. (p. 105)

In sum, adult guidance is one ingredient in the recipe for guided play. Specific interactions with learning materials is another.

Materials: Guided Object Play Uses Manipulatives in Learning

In Chapter 8, I described two interventions to improve children's spatial and math skills. The Building Blocks curriculum uses software and manipulatives to help children progress in learning about specific mathematics concepts, including geometry. The Linear Number Board Game uses materials that children manipulate to learn a particular concept; in this example, the game made it easier for children to learn number skills, including identifying numbers, counting, comparing magnitudes, and estimating using the number line (Ramani & Siegler, 2008).

Beyond engaging children in hands-on activity, the academic goal of manipulatives or other learning materials is to represent an abstract concept in concrete and tangible terms. Though most adults can count without fingers or other tools, young children who are learning to pair an abstract number word with its quantitative concept are helped by having a tangible "thing" to count. And just as unstructured free play is not necessarily beneficial, remember the idea that manipulatives are not a panacea (Clements & McMillen, 1996). Children may just as likely find them distracting as useful in their learning. Rather, the crucial feature of manipulatives is that they successfully represent the concept to be learned.

To represent abstract concepts, manipulatives must provide cues that remind children of the difficult concept they are striving to automate. By this logic, the closer the manipulative, toy, or game is, in its features or arrangement, to the difficult concept, the more readily the manipulative should help support the learning. Both the Building Blocks curriculum and the Linear Number Board Game were designed with this logic in mind.

In other chapters, I described multiple successful approaches that take advantage of manipulatives and concrete objects in the environment:

In Chapter 4, most motor skills assessments involve using manipulatives.

In Chapter 5, children had better spatial skills when their caregivers talked more about spatial elements of objects and the overall environment.

In Chapter 7, in a book-reading situation, children were helped to remember a story about farm animals by acting it out with miniature farm animal toys.

In Chapter 9, the Minds in Motion after-school curriculum had children practice their executive function, motor, and spatial skills with arts and crafts materials.

There is also strong evidence from a large national sample that manipulatives-based mathematics instruction supports kindergartners' mathematics learning, but not the learning of 1st-graders (Guarino et al., 2013). Whereas kindergartners learned more math when their teachers reported using manipulatives and writing on the chalkboard, 1st-graders learned more when their teachers reported spending classroom time explaining math problems.

These findings are consistent with the idea that relatively younger children benefit from concrete representations of abstract concepts . . . which playing with objects *has the potential* to do. But as I emphasized in Chapter 9, unstructured free play as typically practiced in preschool classrooms is not associated with learning, at least compared with other activities (Chien et al., 2010). This is why adult involvement is so crucial to whether and how guided object play supports learning.

SUCCESSFUL CURRICULA EXPLICITLY TEACH FOUNDATIONAL COGNITIVE SKILLS THROUGH GUIDED OBJECT PLAY

Simply putting children in the same room with attractive or expensive learning materials has not been shown to make a difference in their learning. None of the studies featured in this book found that exposure to materials is all that children need. What's more, some materials must be used in precise ways to show effects on children's learning. For example, only children who "count-on" from their numbered space when playing the Linear Number Board Game improve in their math skills (Laski & Siegler, 2014). Children who count from 1—even if they are on the space marked "10"—didn't learn as much.

Whether to count from 1 or count from the number space on the board is an extremely subtle variation. Yet the change makes a big difference. If the interventions I reviewed in this book have in common that they use manipulatives, it is also true that researchers or school staff were taught to use the manipulatives in a specific way. And these programs made sure that children were given adequate time to practice their skills on a regular basis, meaning multiple times per week.

In addition to using materials, the Building Blocks early childhood mathematics curriculum described in Chapter 8 and the Minds in Motion after-school curriculum described in Chapter 9 shared several important features in common:

- Both programs were 5 to 6 months in length, with children participating regularly, four times per week, for 10–45 minutes at a time.
- Both programs involved adults working closely with children in small-group settings, guiding their activities and use of materials.
- Both programs included *constructional activities*, where children made their own versions of provided examples, using a range of materials in two and three dimensions.

- Both programs improved children's spatial skills, with additional improvements to oral language for Building Blocks (Sarama et al., 2012), and to EF and classroom behavior for Minds in Motion (Brock et al., in press).

Essentially, I'm proposing that teachers should give explicit attention and support to children's foundational cognitive skills through teaching children how to use materials and games.

This rationale derives from the work of Carol Connor of the University of California–Irvine and Fred Morrison of the University of Michigan, who are experts on literacy acquisition among young children. They note that any learning activity can be described according to "whether instruction is explicit or implicit in promoting growth of a particular skill" (Connor, Morrison, & Katch, 2004, p. 308). In other words, skills can be the explicit or deliberate focus of an educational activity, or an implicit or incidental focus of the activity (Connor et al., 2004; Foorman, Francis, Fletcher, Schatschneider, & Mehta, 1998).

To explain the difference in an activity's explicit or implicit skills focus, consider Connor et al.'s (2004) example of a whole-group book reading where the teacher reads the book and engages the children in discussing what happened. This activity is explicitly focused on comprehension, because teachers intentionally direct children's attention to topics such as the meaning of events, the order in which they happened, and making predictions during the book reading. At the same time, children may pick up other information, such as the sound of a letter or how to hold a book, "in an implicit or incidental fashion" (p. 309)—in other words, accidentally.

Connor and Morrison and colleagues have conducted extensive correlational and experimental research to understand explicit and implicit learning activities in relation to preschool and elementary students' literacy acquisition. Their studies since 2004 show that different children benefit from different types of activities, depending on the skill levels with which they begin school (Connor et al., 2004; Connor et al., 2010; Connor, Morrison, & Slominski, 2006). Specifically, implicit activities are appropriate and beneficial for children with the highest skill levels. In contrast, for children who start the school year with low levels of either decoding or comprehension, explicit activities are the most beneficial in promoting those outcomes.

Applied to foundational cognitive skills, children who enter school with low levels of EF, motor skills, or spatial skills may benefit most from explicit attempts to improve them. Yet, for the most part, EF, motor skills, and spatial skills remain an implicit or incidental focus of early childhood lessons, curricula, and policy. That is, although many preschool and kindergarten activities require children to focus and shift their attention while controlling their impulses (executive function); to arrange their bodies, hands, and materials appropriately for learning (motor skills); and to make sense of spatial information (spatial skills), the most common unstructured play activities do not provide enough scaffolding for children to stretch their skills. At the risk of sounding like a broken record, here is where guided object play comes in.

SUMMARY AND OVERALL CONCLUSION

Guided object play fits the early childhood classroom, where play is considered developmentally appropriate practice (Bredekamp & Copple, 2009). More guidance than teachers typically provide is needed to ensure that children take the most from each learning opportunity, however (Chien et al., 2010; Weisberg et al., 2013).

Guided object play can be modified to fit children of varying language backgrounds and fine motor skill levels (Cottone & Chen, 2013; Weisberg et al., 2013). Appropriate modifications to material complexity increase the opportunities for children to learn with caregivers in guided (scaffolded) interactions, and are consistent with studies reviewed throughout this book that demonstrate how to improve the foundational cognitive skills of EF, motor skills, and spatial skills.

Like the subtle differences in how the Linear Number Board Game may be played, the shift in mindset that research encourages is subtle. Instead of inviting the easy conclusion that "free play is good for children," the studies I have reviewed should lead early childhood professionals to ask more questions, such as the following:

- What types of play are children in my classroom engaged in? (Refer to Table 9.1 for types of play.)
- What skills do individual children need to practice? (Refer to Table P.1 for different foundational cognitive skills.)
- What materials and support can I provide so they practice those skills?

I would need another book to provide an adequate answer to the third question, because there is no single activity, lesson, or material that will magically teach children foundational cognitive skills, or make them ready for school.

Like medicine, education sometimes suffers from a search for a silver bullet. Humans enjoy simple answers. But educating young children is a complex process to be engaged with over time. Every child enters the classroom with different experiences, proclivities, strengths, and challenges. Understanding what a particular child needs takes time, attention, and dedication from early childhood professionals, many of whom are underpaid and experiencing their own stress even as they strive to help children adapt to school (Friedman-Krauss, Raver, Neuspiel, & Kinsel, 2014).

Supporting children's school readiness should not be left to teachers alone. This sacred work needs social resources in the context of healthy families, neighborhoods, communities, and schools. Supporting school readiness also needs financial investment and smart policy from our leaders. In the United States, we expect tremendous things from teachers, without appreciating the systemwide shifts that must occur if we are to invest our nation's vast financial and social resources adequately in young people (Penner, 2014; Wright, 2011).

One helpful shift needs to occur in the research community, to better communicate with practitioners established results that can inform effective early childhood practices (Tseng, 2012). There is empirical support from large studies with children across the United States and in other countries that the following are critical ingredients in the recipe for school readiness:

- High-quality, one-on-one, and small-group *interactions* among adults and children
- *Materials*, including computer tools, designed with particular skills in mind
- *Time* for children to practice foundational cognitive skills explicitly
- Opportunities for both free play and *guided object play*, such as constructional tasks where adults help children make models in 2D and 3D, and then play with materials as they wish

Even with better communication about research, guided object play and other effective practices will not just magically appear in preschool and early elementary classrooms, which are tending toward more time in direct academic instruction (Bassok et al., 2016). Shifts in the way that future teachers are trained, funding for such preparation, and continuing education are also needed.

Just as it's unfair to burden teachers with the sole responsibility for children's learning, behavior, and outcomes—as though children do not exist as learning creatures until they start school—teachers should not be held responsible for making these systemic changes.

Instead, all of us with a stake in early childhood development and education need investment, including research on the learning progressions of the foundational cognitive skills, similar to the work that reveals how young children learn mathematics concepts like geometry (Clements & Sarama, 2008; Clements et al., 2004). Professionals also need valid and economical assessments to supplement the teacher ratings that are so widely used (Mashburn et al., 2006).

Finally, from our federal and state leaders, we need commitments to the healthy development of young children and families. In the polarized U.S. political climate, some good news is that the bipartisan work that does happen advances long-standing social policies, especially those designed with the well-being of many different groups of children and their families in mind (Haskins, 2016).

Meanwhile, we have a long way to go before every child has access to high-quality early education that includes positive teacher–child relationships, engaging and age-appropriate learning materials, and adequate time to play with materials while learning from adults, peers, and self. With these key ingredients, researchers, teachers, and families can foster school readiness in every child.

By the End of the School Year . . .

You feel so proud of the children in your class. Aja, Nadia, Jean and Eli, Michael and Charlie, Miriam, Jack, Alicia, and Marcus have all grown so much this year.

Nadia created several Play-Doh creatures, and the children made a theater area for dramatic displays with the creatures. Jean and Eli, the experts at pretend play, put on the most entertaining "Play-Doh People" shows. And Miriam knows all the classes' board game rules by heart, in part because she has played each game many times with the Play-Doh People.

Marcus's favorite activity was making any type of design he could bring home to his grandmother. Come to think of it, all the children enjoyed taking home their designs. It did get expensive to buy the additional materials, but you noticed that it's easier to use spatial vocabulary words when children are playing with certain materials. Once you help them get situated in their own space, most of the children seem to lose track of time because they become so engaged with making their designs.

The Creative Model Center, where children first make a model that they can pick from a variety of choices and then play with the materials provided, has become the class favorite. When it's his turn to choose a place to play, Jack sometimes chooses the Creative Model Center over the blocks area. He and Alicia have become chums and work happily next to each other.

Overall, you feel pleased with how your first year of teaching preschool turned out. You stretched yourself to meet the challenge of providing your children with as much individual and small-group support during play as you could and feel proud of your many successes. Most important, in fostering your children's EF, motor skills, and spatial skills, you helped the children—and yourself—relish the splendid and sometimes surprising process of learning.

References

AAP Council on Early Childhood & AAP Council on School Health. (2016). The pediatrician's role in optimizing school readiness. *Pediatrics, 138*(3). doi:10.1542/peds.2016-2293

Ackerman, D. J., & Friedman-Krauss, A. H. (2017). Preschoolers' executive function: Importance, contributors, research needs and assessment options. *ETS Research Report Series.* doi:10.1002/ets2.12148

Administration on Children Youth and Families/Head Start Bureau. (2003). *Head Start outcomes framework: The Head Start path to positive child outcomes.* Washington, DC: U.S. Department of Health and Human Services.

Administration on Children Youth and Families/Head Start Bureau. (2010). *The Head Start child development and early learning framework: Promoting positive outcomes in early childhood programs serving children 3–5 years old.* Washington, DC: U.S. Department of Health and Human Services.

Administration on Children Youth and Families/Head Start Bureau. (2015). *Head Start early learning outcomes framework: Ages birth to five.* Washington, DC: Department of Health and Human Services.

Adolph, K. E. (2015, March). Good behavior: Coding, sharing, and repurposing video. Paper presented at the Society for Research in Child Development Biennial Meeting, Philadelphia, PA.

Adolph, K. E., & Berger, S. E. (2006). Motor development. In D. Kuhn, R. S. Siegler, W. Damon, & R. M. Lerner (Eds.), *Handbook of child psychology: Vol. 2, Cognition, perception, and language* (6th ed., pp. 161–213). Hoboken, NJ: John Wiley & Sons Inc.

Alfieri, L., Brooks, P. J., Aldrich, N. J., & Tenenbaum, H. R. (2011). Does discovery-based instruction enhance learning? *Journal of Educational Psychology, 103*(1), 1–18. doi:10.1037/a0021017; 10.1037/a0021017.supp (Supplemental)

American Academy of Pediatrics. (2016). Media and young minds. *Pediatrics.* doi:10.1542/peds.2016-2591

American Occupational Therapy Association (AOTA). (2014). Occupational therapy practice framework: Domain and process (3rd ed.). *American Journal of Occupational Therapy, 68*(Supplement_1), S1–S48. doi:10.5014/ajot.2014.682006

Arlin, M. (1979). Teacher transitions can disrupt time flow in classrooms. *American Educational Research Journal, 16*(1), 42–56.

Baddeley, A., Gathercole, S., & Papagno, C. (1998). The phonological loop as a language learning device. *Psychological Review, 105*(1), 158–173. doi:10.1037/0033-295X.105.1.158

Barnett, W. S., Jung, K., Yarosz, D. J., Thomas, J., Hornbeck, A., Stechuk, R., & Burns, S. (2008). Educational effects of the Tools of the Mind curriculum: A randomized trial. *Early Childhood Research Quarterly, 23*(3), 299–313.

Bassok, D., Latham, S., & Rorem, A. (2016). Is kindergarten the new first grade? *AERA Open, 2*(1). doi:10.1177/2332858415616358

Becker, D. R., McClelland, M. M., Loprinzi, P., & Trost, S. G. (2014). Physical activity, self-regulation, and early academic achievement in preschool children. *Early Education and Development, 25*(1), 56–70. doi:10.1080/10409289.2013.780505

Becker, D. R., Miao, A., Duncan, R., & McClelland, M. M. (2014). Behavioral self-regulation and executive function both predict visuomotor skills and early academic achievement. *Early Childhood Research Quarterly, 29*(4), 411–424. doi:10.1016/j.ecresq.2014.04.014

Beery, K. E., & Beery, N. A. (2010). *Beery VMI administration, scoring, and teaching manual* (6th ed.). Bloomington, MN: Pearson.

Beery, K. E., Buktenica, N. A., & Beery, N. A. (2010). *Beery-Buktenica developmental test of visual-motor integration*, 6th ed. (BEERY™ VMI). San Antonio, TX: Pearson.

Berenhaus, M., Oakhill, J., & Rusted, J. (2015). When kids act out: A comparison of embodied methods to improve children's memory for a story. *Journal of Research in Reading, 38*(4), 331–343. doi:10.1111/1467-9817.12039

Berkowicz, J., & Myers, A. (2017). Spatial skills: A neglected dimension of early STEM education. Retrieved from blogs.edweek.org/edweek/leadership_360/2017/02/spatial_skills_a_neglected_dimension_of_early_stem_education.html

Berninger, V., Yates, C., Cartwright, A., Rutberg, J., Remy, E., & Abbott, R. (1992). Lower-level developmental skills in beginning writing. *Reading and Writing, 4*(3), 257–280. doi:10.1007/bf01027151

Best, J. R., Theim, K. R., Gredysa, D. M., Stein, R. I., Welch, R. R., Saelens, B. E., . . . Wilfley, D. E. (2012). Behavioral economic predictors of overweight children's weight loss. *Journal of Consulting and Clinical Psychology, 80*(6), 1086–1096. doi:10.1037/a0029827

Bierman, K. L., Nix, R. L., Greenberg, M. T., Blair, C., & Domitrovich, C. E. (2008). Executive functions and school readiness intervention: Impact, moderation, and mediation in the Head Start REDI program. *Development and Psychopathology, 20*(3), 821–843. doi:10.1017/S0954579408000394

Blair, C., Protzko, J., & Ursache, A. (2011). Self-regulation and early literacy. In S. B. Neuman & D. K. Dickinson (Eds.), *Handbook of early literacy research* (Vol. 3, pp. 20–35). New York, NY: Guilford.

Blair, C., & Raver, C. C. (2012). Child development in the context of adversity: Experiential canalization of brain and behavior. *American Psychologist, 67*(4), 309–318.

Blair, C., & Raver, C. C. (2015). School readiness and self-regulation: A developmental psychobiological approach. *Annual Review of Psychology, 3*(66), 711–731. doi:10.1146/annurev-psych-010814-015221

Blair, C., & Razza, R. P. (2007). Relating effortful control, executive function, and false belief understanding to emerging math and literacy ability in kindergarten. *Child Development, 78*(2), 647–663. doi:10.1111/j.1467-8624.2007.01019.x

Blair, C., Ursache, A., Greenberg, M., & Vernon-Feagans, L. (2015). Multiple aspects of self-regulation uniquely predict mathematics but not letter–word knowledge in the early elementary grades. *Developmental Psychology, 51*(4), 459–472. doi:10.1037/a0038813

Bodrova, E., & Leong, D. J. (2006). Self-regulation as a key to school readiness: How early childhood teachers can promote this critical competency. In M. Zaslow & I. Martinez-Beck (Eds.), *Critical issues in early childhood professional development* (pp. 203–224). Baltimore, MD: Brookes.

Bodrova, E., & Leong, D. (2007). *Tools of the Mind: The Vygotskian approach to early childhood education* (2nd ed.). Columbus, OH: Merrill/Prentice Hall.

Bonawitz, E., Shafto, P., Gweon, H., Goodman, N. D., Spelke, E., & Schulz, L. (2011). The double-edged sword of pedagogy: Instruction limits spontaneous exploration and discovery. *Cognition, 120*(3), 322–330. doi:10.1016/j.cognition.2010.10.001

Bracken, B. (1998). *The Bracken basic concepts scale—Revised.* San Antonio, TX: The Psychological Corporation.

Bredekamp, S., & Copple, C. (2009). *Developmentally appropriate practice in early childhood programs serving children from birth through age 8* (3rd ed.). Washington, DC: National Association for the Education of Young Children.

Brock, L. L., Murrah, W. M., Cottone, E. A., Mashburn, A. J., & Grissmer, D. W. (in press). An after school intervention targeting executive function and visuospatial skills also improves classroom behavior. *International Journal of Behavioral Development.*

Bronfenbrenner, U., & Morris, P. A. (2006). *The bioecological model of human development.* Hoboken, NJ: John Wiley & Sons Inc.

Bronson, M. B. (1994). The usefulness of an observational measure of young children's social and mastery behaviors in early childhood classrooms. *Early Childhood Research Quarterly, 9*(1), 19–43.

Bruininks, R. H., & Bruininks, B. D. (2005). *Bruininks-Oseretsky test of motor proficiency, 2nd ed.* (BOT™-2). San Antonio, TX: Pearson.

Bulotsky-Shearer, R. J., Fantuzzo, J. W., & McDermott, P. A. (2008). An investigation of classroom situational dimensions of emotional and behavioral adjustment and cognitive and social outcomes for Head Start children. *Developmental Psychology, 44*(1), 139–154.

Burdette, H. L., & Whitaker, R. C. (2005). Resurrecting free play in young children: Looking beyond fitness and fatness to attention, affiliation, and affect. *Archives of Pediatrics & Adolescent Medicine, 159*(1), 46–50.

Burghardt, G. M. (2012). Defining and recognizing play. In A. Pellegrini (Ed.), *Oxford handbook of the development of play* (pp. 9–18).New York, NY: Oxford University Press.

Burrage, M. S., Cameron Ponitz, C., McCready, E. A., Shah, P., Sims, B. C., Jewkes, A. M., & Morrison, F. J. (2008). Age- and schooling-related effects on executive functions in young children: A natural experiment. *Child Neuropsychology, 14,* 510–524. doi:10.1080/09297040701756917

Burton, A. W., & Dancisak, M. J. (2000). Grip form and graphomotor control in preschool children. *American Journal of Occupational Therapy, 54*(1), 9–17. doi:10.5014/ajot.54.1.9

Burton, A. W., & Rodgerson, R. W. (2001). New perspectives on the assessment of movement skills and motor abilities. *Adapted Physical Activity Quarterly, 18*(4), 347–365.

Bus, A. G., Takacs, Z. K., & Kegel, C. A. T. (2015). Affordances and limitations of electronic storybooks for young children's emergent literacy. *Developmental Review, 35,* 79–97. doi:10.1016/j.dr.2014.12.004

Cabrera, N. J., Shannon, J. D., & Tamis-LeMonda, C. (2007). Fathers' influence on their children's cognitive and emotional development: From toddlers to pre-K. *Applied Developmental Science, 11*(4), 208–213.

Calkins, S. D. (2004). Early attachment processes and the development of emotional self-regulation. In R. F. Baumeister & K. D. Vohs (Eds.), *Handbook of self-regulation: Research, theory, and applications* (pp. 324–339). New York, NY: Guilford.

Calkins, S. D. (2007). The emergence of self-regulation: Biological and behavioral control mechanisms supporting toddler competencies. In C. A. Brownell & C. B. Kopp (Eds.), *Socioemotional development in the toddler years: Transitions and transformations* (pp. 261–284). New York, NY: Guilford.

Cameron, C. E., Brock, L. L., Hatfield, B. E., Cottone, E. A., Rubinstein, E., LoCasale-Crouch, J., & Grissmer, D. W. (2015). Visuomotor integration and inhibitory control compensate for each other in school readiness. *Developmental Psychology, 51*(11), 1529–1543. doi:10.1037/a0039740

Cameron, C. E., Brock, L. L., Murrah, W. M., Bell, L. H., Worzalla, S. L., Grissmer, D. W., & Morrison, F. J. (2012). Fine motor skills and executive function both contribute to kindergarten achievement. *Child Development, 83*(4), 1229–1244. doi:10.1111/j.1467-8624.2012.01768.x

Cameron, C. E., Chen, W.-B., Blodgett, J., Cottone, E. A., Mashburn, A. J., Brock, L. L., & Grissmer, D. W. (2012). Preliminary validation of the Motor Skills Rating Scale. *Journal of Psychoeducational Assessment, 30*(6), 555–566. doi:10.1177/0734282911435462

Cameron, C. E., Cottone, E. A., Murrah, W. M., & Grissmer, D. W. (2016). How are motor skills linked to children's school performance and academic achievement? *Child Development Perspectives, 10*(2). doi:10.1111/cdep.12168

Cameron, C. E., Grimm, K. J., Steele, J. S., Castro-Schilo, L., & Grissmer, D. W. (2015). Nonlinear Gompertz curve models of achievement gaps in mathematics and reading. *Journal of Educational Psychology, 107*(3), 789–804. doi:10.1037/edu0000009

Cameron, C. E., & Morrison, F. J. (2011). Teacher activity orienting predicts preschoolers' academic and self-regulatory skills. *Early Education & Development, 22*(4), 620–648. doi:10.1080/10409280903544405

Cameron Ponitz, C. E., McClelland, M. M., Jewkes, A. M., Connor, C. M., Farris, C. L., & Morrison, F. J. (2008). Touch your toes! Developing a direct measure of behavioral regulation in early childhood. *Early Childhood Research Quarterly, 23*(2), 141–158. doi:10.1016/j.ecresq.2007.01.004

Cameron Ponitz, C. E., McClelland, M. M., Matthews, J. S., & Morrison, F. J. (2009). A structured observation of behavioral self-regulation and its contribution to kindergarten outcomes. *Developmental Psychology, 45*(3), 605–619. doi:10.1037/a0015365

Cameron Ponitz, C. E., Rimm-Kaufman, S. E., Grimm, K. J., & Curby, T. W. (2009). Kindergarten classroom quality, behavioral engagement, and reading achievement. *School Psychology Review, 38*(1), 102–120.

Campos, J. J., Anderson, D. I., Barbu-Roth, M. A., Hubbard, E. M., Hertenstein, M. J., & Witherington, D. (2000). Travel broadens the mind. *Infancy, 1*(2), 149–219.

Carlson, A. G., Rowe, E., & Curby, T. R. (2013). Disentangling fine motor skills' relations to academic achievement: The relative contributions of visual-spatial integration and visual-motor coordination. *Journal of Genetic Psychology,* *174*(5–6), 514–533. doi:10.1080/00221325.2012.717122

Carlson, S. M. (2005). Developmentally sensitive measures of executive function in preschool children. *Developmental Neuropsychology, 28*(2), 595–616. doi:10.1207/s15326942dn2802_3

Carlson, S. M., & Harrod, J. (2013). *The executive function scale for preschoolers: Validation phase.* Paper presented at the Society for Research in Child Development, Seattle, WA.

Case, R. (1996). VIII. Summary and conclusion. Reconceptualizing the nature of children's conceptual structures and their development in middle childhood. *Monographs of the Society for Research in Child Development, 61*(1–2), 189–214. doi:10.1111/j.1540-5834.1996.tb00542.x

Chaddock, L., Erickson, K. I., Prakash, R. S., VanPatter, M., Voss, M. W., Pontifex, M. B., . . . Kramer, A. F. (2010). Basal ganglia volume is associated with aerobic fitness in preadolescent children. *Developmental Neuroscience, 32*(3), 249–256.

Chaddock-Heyman, L., Hillman, C. H., Cohen, N. J., & Kramer, A. F. (2014). III. The importance of physical activity and aerobic fitness for cognitive control and memory in children. *Monographs of the Society for Research in Child Development, 79*(4), 25–50. doi:10.1111/mono.12129

Chen, W.-B., Grimm, K. J., Grissmer, D. W., & Gregory, A. (2010). The transactional interplay between parent-child interaction quality, fine motor development, and cognitive development in early childhood (Unpublished doctoral dissertation). Charlottesville, VA: University of Virginia.

Cheng, Y.-L., & Mix, K. S. (2014). Spatial training improves children's mathematics ability. *Journal of Cognition and Development, 15*(1), 2–11.

Chien, N. C., Howes, C., Burchinal, M., Pianta, R. C., Ritchie, S., Bryant, D. M., . . . Barbarin, O. A. (2010). Children's classroom engagement and school readiness gains in prekindergarten. *Child Development, 81*(5), 1534–1549. doi:10.1111/j.1467-8624.2010.01490.x

Choe, D. E., Olson, S. L., & Sameroff, A. J. (2013). The interplay of externalizing problems and physical and inductive discipline during childhood. *Developmental Psychology, 49*(11), 2029–2039. doi:10.1037/a0032054

Clements, D. H., & McMillen, S. (1996). Rethinking "concrete" manipulatives. *Teaching Children Mathematics, 2*(5), 270–279.

Clements, D. H., & Sarama, J. (2007). Effects of a preschool mathematics curriculum: Summative research on the Building Blocks project. *Journal for Research in Mathematics Education, 38*(2), 136–163. doi:10.2307/30034954

Clements, D. H., & Sarama, J. (2008). Experimental evaluation of the effects of a research-based preschool mathematics curriculum. *American Educational Research Journal, 45*(2), 443–494. doi:10.3102/0002831207312908

Clements, D. H., & Sarama, J. (2011). Early childhood teacher education: The case of geometry. *Journal of Mathematics Teacher Education, 14*(2), 133–148. doi:10.1007/s10857-011-9173-0

Clements, D. H., Sarama, J., Spitler, M. E., Lange, A. A., & Wolfe, C. B. (2011). Mathematics learned by young children in an intervention based on learning trajectories: A large-scale cluster randomized trial. *Journal for Research in Mathematics Education, 42*(2), 127–166. doi:10.5951/jresematheduc.42.2.0127

Clements, D. H., Wilson, D. C., & Sarama, J. (2004). Young children's composition of geometric figures: A learning trajectory. *Mathematical Thinking and Learning, 6*(2), 163–184. doi:10.1207/s15327833mtl0602_5

Connor, C. M., Cameron Ponitz, C. E., Phillips, B. M., Travis, Q. M., Glasney, S., & Morrison, F. J. (2010). First graders' literacy and self-regulation gains: The effect of individualizing student instruction. *Journal of School Psychology, 48*(5), 433–455.

Connor, C. M., Morrison, F. J., & Katch, L. E. (2004). Beyond the reading wars: Exploring the effect of child-instruction interactions on growth in early reading. *Scientific Studies of Reading, 8*(4), 305–336.

Connor, C. M., Morrison, F. J., & Slominski, L. (2006). Preschool instruction and children's emergent literacy growth. *Journal of Educational Psychology, 98*(4), 665–689.

Cottone, E. A., & Chen, W.-B. (2013). *Minds in Motion, unpublished after-school fine motor skills curriculum*. Charlottesville, VA: University of Virginia.

Crescentini, C., Fabbro, F., & Urgesi, C. (2014). Mental spatial transformations of objects and bodies: Different developmental trajectories in children from 7 to 11 years of age. *Developmental Psychology, 50*(2), 370–383. doi:10.1037/a0033627

Curby, T. W., Brock, L. L., & Hamre, B. K. (2013). Teachers' emotional support consistency predicts children's achievement gains and social skills. *Early Education & Development, 24*(3), 292–309. doi:10.1080/10409289.2012.665760

Davis, C. L., Tomporowski, P. D., McDowell, J. E., Austin, B. P., Miller, P. H., Yanasak, N. E., . . . Naglieri, J. A. (2011). Exercise improves executive function and achievement and alters brain activation in overweight children: A randomized, controlled trial. *Health Psychology, 30*(1), 91–98. doi:10.1037/a0021766

Davis, E. E., Pitchford, N. J., & Limback, E. (2011). The interrelation between cognitive and motor development in typically developing children aged 4–11 years is underpinned by visual processing and fine manual control. *British Journal of Psychology, 102*(3), 569–584. doi:10.1111/j.2044-8295.2011.02018.x

Deci, E. L., & Ryan, R. M. (2000). The "what" and "why" of goal pursuits: Human needs and the self-determination of behavior. *Psychological Inquiry, 11*(4), 227–268.

Dehaene, S. (1992). Varieties of numerical abilities. *Cognition, 44*(1–2), 1–42. Retrieved from www.ncbi.nlm.nih.gov/pubmed/1511583

Del Giudice, E., Grossi, D., Angelini, R., Crisanti, A. F., Latte, F., Fragassi, N. A., & Trojano, L. (2000). Spatial cognition in children. I. Development of drawing-related (visuospatial and constructional) abilities in preschool and early school years. *Brain & Development, 22*(6), 362–367. doi:10.1016/S0387-7604(00)00158-3

De Lisi, R., & Wolford, J. L. (2002). Improving children's mental rotation accuracy with computer game playing. *Journal of Genetic Psychology, 163*(3), 272–282. doi:10.1080/00221320209598683

Denham, S. A. (2006). Social-emotional competence as support for school readiness: What is it and how do we assess it? *Early Education and Development, 17*(1), 57–89. doi:10.1207/s15566935eed1701_4

Dewey, D., & Wilson, B. N. (2001). Developmental coordination disorder: What is it? *Physical & Occupational Therapy in Pediatrics, 20*(2–3), 5–27.

Diamond, A. (2000). Close interrelation of motor development and cognitive development and of the cerebellum and prefrontal cortex. *Child Development, 71*(1), 44–56. doi:10.1111/1467-8624.00117

Diamond, A. (2012). Activities and programs that improve children's executive functions. *Current Directions in Psychological Science, 21*(5), 335–341. doi:10.1177/0963721412453722

Diamond, A. (2013). Executive functions. *Annual Review of Psychology, 64*(1), 135–168. doi:10.1146/annurev-psych-113011-143750

Diamond, A. (2016). Why improving and assessing executive functions early in life is critical. In J. A. Griffin, P. McCardle, & L. S. Freund (Eds.), *Executive function in preschool-age children: Integrating measurement, neurodevelopment, and translational research* (pp. 11–43). Washington, DC: American Psychological Association.

Diamond, A., Kirkham, N., & Amso, D. (2002). Conditions under which young children can hold two rules in mind and inhibit a prepotent response. *Developmental Psychology, 38*(3), 352–362.

Diamond, A., & Lee, K. (2011). Interventions shown to aid executive function development in children 4 to 12 years old. *Science, 333*(6045), 959–964. doi:10.1126/science.1204529

Dirksen, T., De Lussanet, M. H., Zentgraf, K., Slupinski, L., & Wagner, H. (2016). Increased throwing accuracy improves children's catching performance in a ball-catching task from the Movement Assessment Battery (MABC-2). *Frontiers in Psychology, 7*, 1122. doi:10.3389/fpsyg.2016.01122

Dishion, T. J., & Tipsord, J. M. (2011). Peer contagion in child and adolescent social and emotional development. *Annual Review of Psychology, 62*, 189–214. Retrieved from www.ncbi.nlm.nih.gov/pmc/articles/PMC3523739/

Downer, J. T., Booren, L. M., Lima, O. K., Luckner, A. E., & Pianta, R. C. (2011). The Individualized Classroom Assessment Scoring System (inCLASS): Preliminary reliability and validity of a system for observing preschoolers' competence in classroom interactions. *Early Childhood Research Quarterly, 25*(1), 1–16.

Dweck, C. (2006). *Mindset: The new psychology of success.* New York, NY: Ballantine Books.

Early, D. M., Barbarin, O., Bryant, D., Burchinal, M., Chang, F., Clifford, R., . . . Barnett, W. S. (2005). *Pre-kindergarten in eleven states: NCEDL's multi-state study of pre-kindergarten & study of state-wide early education programs (SWEEP): Preliminary descriptive report.* Chapel Hill: The University of North Carolina, FPG Child Development Institute, NCEDL. Retrieved from www.fpg.unc.edu/~ncedl/pdfs/SWEEP_MS_summary_final.pdf

Ehrlich, S. B., Levine, S. C., & Goldin-Meadow, S. (2006). The importance of gesture in children's spatial reasoning. *Developmental Psychology, 42*(6), 1259–1268. doi:10.1037/0012-1649.42.6.1259

Eisenberg, N., & Spinrad, T. L. (2004). Emotion-related regulation: Sharpening the definition. *Child Development, 75*(2), 334–339.

Farran, D. C., Wilson, S. J., Meador, D., Norvell, J., & Nesbitt, K. (2015). *Experimental evaluation of the Tools of the Mind pre-K curriculum: Technical report* (Working paper). Retrieved from my.vanderbilt.edu/toolsofthemindevaluation/files/2011/12/Tools-Technical-Report-Final-September-2015.pdf

Feder, K. P., & Majnemer, A. (2007). Handwriting development, competency, and intervention. *Developmental Medicine and Child Neurology, 49*(4), 312–317.

Feldon, D. F. (2007). Cognitive load and classroom teaching: The double-edged sword of automaticity. *Educational Psychologist, 42*(3), 123–137. doi:10.1080 /00461520701416173

Fisher, K. R., Hirsh-Pasek, K., Golinkoff, R. M., & Gryfe, S. G. (2008). Conceptual split? Parents' and experts' perceptions of play in the 21st century. *Journal of Applied Developmental Psychology, 29*(4), 305–316. doi:10.1016/j.appdev .2008.04.006

Floyer-Lea, A., & Matthews, P. M. (2004). Changing brain networks for visuomotor control with increased movement automaticity. *Journal of Neurophysiology, 92*(4), 2405–2412. doi:10.1152/jn.01092.2003

Foorman, B. R., Francis, D. J., Fletcher, J. M., Schatschneider, C., & Mehta, P. (1998). The role of instruction in learning to read: Preventing reading failure in at-risk children. *Journal of Educational Psychology, 90*(1), 37–55.

Fosnot, C. T. (2005). *Constructivism: Theory, perspectives, and practice* (2nd ed.). New York, NY: Teachers College Press.

Friedman, N. P., Miyake, A., Young, S. E., DeFries, J. C., Corley, R. P., & Hewitt, J. K. (2008). Individual differences in executive functions are almost entirely genetic in origin. *Journal of Experimental Psychology: General, 137*(2), 201–225. doi:10.1037/0096-3445.137.2.201

Friedman-Krauss, A. H., Raver, C. C., Neuspiel, J. M., & Kinsel, J. (2014). Child behavior problems, teacher executive functions, and teacher stress in Head Start classrooms. *Early Education and Development, 25*(5), 681–702. doi:10.1080 /10409289.2013.825190

Fuchs, L. S., Geary, D. C., Compton, D. L., Fuchs, D., Hamlett, C. L., Seethaler, P. M., . . . Schatschneider, C. (2010). Do different types of school mathematics development depend on different constellations of numerical versus general cognitive abilities? *Developmental Psychology, 46*(6), 1731–1746. doi:10.1037 /a0020662

Fuhs, M. W., Nesbitt, K. T., Farran, D. C., & Dong, N. (2014). Longitudinal associations between executive functioning and academic skills across content areas. *Developmental Psychology, 50*(6), 1698–1709. doi:10.1037/a0036633

Gamoran, A. (2015). *New challenges for research on youth inequality.* Paper presented at the Curry Research Lectureship Series Invited Presentation, April 10, 2015, Charlottesville, VA.

Gathercole, S. E., Pickering, S. J., Ambridge, B., & Wearing, H. (2004). The structure of working memory from 4 to 15 years of age. *Developmental Psychology, 40*(2), 177–190. doi:10.1037/0012-1649.40.2.177

Gilliam, W. S., Maupin, A. N., Reyes, C. R., Accavitti, M., & Shic, F. (2016). Do early educators' implicit biases regarding sex and race relate to behavior expectations and recommendations of preschool expulsions and suspensions? (A research study brief). New Haven, CT: Yale University Child Study Center. Retrieved from ziglercenter.yale.edu/publications/Preschool%20Implicit%20Bias %20Policy%20Brief_final_9_26_276766_5379_v1.pdf

Glenberg, A. M., Brown, M., & Levin, J. R. (2007). Enhancing comprehension in small reading groups using a manipulation strategy. *Contemporary Educational Psychology, 32*(3), 389–399.

Glenberg, A. M., Gutierrez, T., Levin, J. R., Japuntich, S., & Kaschak, M. P. (2004). Activity and imagined activity can enhance young children's reading comprehension. *Journal of Educational Psychology, 96*(3), 424–436.

Goh, T. L. (2017). Children's physical activity and on-task behavior following active academic lessons. *Quest, 69*(2), 177–186. doi:10.1080/00336297.2017 .1290533

Golden, N. H., Schneider, M., & Wood, C. (2016). Preventing obesity and eating disorders in adolescents. *Pediatrics.* doi:10.1542/peds.2016-1649

Greenberg, M. T., Weissberg, R. P., O'Brien, M. U., Zins, J. E., Fredericks, L., Resnik, H., & Elias, M. J. (2003). Enhancing school-based prevention and youth development through coordinated social, emotional, and academic learning. *American Psychologist, 58*(6), 466–474.

Gresham, F. M., & Elliott, S. N. (2008). *Social Skills Improvement System.* San Antonio, TX: Pearson.

Grissmer, D. W., & Eiseman, E. (2008). Can gaps in the quality of early environments and non-cognitive skills help explain persisting Black-White achievement gaps? In K. Magnuson & J. Waldfogel (Eds.), *Steady gains and stalled progress: Inequality and the Black-White test score gap* (pp. 139–180). New York, NY: Russell Sage Foundation.

Grissmer, D. W., Grimm, K. J., Aiyer, S. M., Murrah, W. M., & Steele, J. S. (2010). Fine motor skills and early comprehension of the world: Two new school readiness indicators. *Developmental Psychology, 46*(5), 1008–1017. doi:10.1037 /a0020104; 10.1037/a0020104.supp (Supplemental)

Grolnick, W. S., & Farkas, M. (2002). Parenting and the development of children's self-regulation. In M. H. Bornstein (Ed.), *Handbook of parenting: Practical issues in parenting* (2nd ed., Vol. 5, pp. 89–110). Mahwah, NJ: Lawrence Erlbaum.

Grolnick, W. S., & Ryan, R. M. (1989). Parent styles associated with children's self-regulation and competence in school. *Journal of Educational Psychology, 81*(2), 143–154.

Guarino, C., Dieterle, S. G., Bargagliotti, A. E., & Mason, W. M. (2013). What can we learn about effective early mathematics teaching? A framework for estimating causal effects using longitudinal survey data. *Journal of Research on Educational Effectiveness, 6*(2), 164–198. doi:10.1080/19345747.2012.706695

Hammill, D., Goodman, L., & Wiederholt, J. L. (1974). Visual-motor processes: Can we train them? *The Reading Teacher, 27*(5), 469–478.

Hamre, B. K., Hatfield, B., Pianta, R., & Jamil, F. (2013). Evidence for general and domain-specific elements of teacher–child interactions: Associations with preschool children's development. *Child Development, 85*(3), 1257–1274. doi:10.1111/cdev.12184

Hamre, B. K., & Pianta, R. C. (2001). Early teacher-child relationships and the trajectory of children's school outcomes through eighth grade. *Child Development, 72*(2), 625–638. doi:10.1111/1467-8624.00301

Hamre, B. K., & Pianta, R. C. (2005). Can instructional and emotional support in the first-grade classroom make a difference for children at risk of school failure? *Child Development, 76*(5), 949–967. doi:10.1111/j.1467-8624.2005.00889.x

Hamre, B. K., Pianta, R. C., Downer, J. T., & Mashburn, A. J. (2008). Teachers' perceptions of conflict with young students: Looking beyond problem behaviors. *Social Development, 17*(1), 115–136.

Harter, S., & Pike, R. (1984). The pictorial scale of perceived competence and social acceptance for young children. *Child Development, 55*(6), 1969–1982. doi:10.2307/1129772

Haskins, R. (2016, October 24). Under the radar: Getting social policy done in a divided Washington. The Brookings Institute. Retrieved from www.brookings.edu /opinions/under-the-radar-getting-social-policy-done-in-a-divided-washington/

Henderson, S. E., Sugden, D. A., & Barnett, A. (2007). *Movement Assessment Battery for Children—Second Edition (Movement ABC-2).* San Antonio, TX: Pearson.

Ho, C. A. (2011). *Major developmental characteristics of children's name writing and relationships with fine motor skills and emergent literacy skills* (Unpublished doctoral dissertation). University of Michigan. Retrieved from deepblue .lib.umich.edu/handle/2027.42/84436

Huizinga, M., Dolan, C. V., & van der Molen, M. W. (2006). Age-related change in executive function: Developmental trends and a latent variable analysis. *Neuropsychologia, 44*(11), 2017–2036. doi:10.1016/j.neuropsychologia.2006.01.010

Jennings, P. A. (2015). *Mindfulness for teachers: Simple skills for peace and productivity in the classroom.* New York, NY: W. W. Norton & Company.

Jiang, Y., Granja, M. R., & Koball, H. (2017). *Basic facts about low-income children.* New York, NY: National Center for Children in Poverty. Retrieved from nccp.org /publications/pdf/text_1172.pdf

Johnson, R. E., Chang, C. H., & Lord, R. G. (2006). Moving from cognition to behavior: What the research says. *Psychological Bulletin, 132*(3), 381–415. doi:10.1037/0033-2909.132.3.381

Jones, L. B., Rothbart, M. K., & Posner, M. I. (2003). Development of executive attention in preschool children. *Developmental Science, 6*(5), 498–504. doi:10.1111/1467-7687.00307

Justice, L. M., Mashburn, A., Pence, K. L., & Wiggins, A. (2008). Experimental evaluation of a preschool language curriculum: Influence on children's expressive language skills. *Journal of Speech, Language & Hearing Research, 51*(4), 983–1001.

Kaufman, S. B. (2013). Gorillas agree: Human frontal cortex is nothing special. Retrieved from blogs.scientificamerican.com/beautiful-minds/gorillas-agree -human-frontal-cortex-is-nothing-special/

Kephart, N. C. (1964). Perceptual-motor aspects of learning disabilities. *Exceptional Children, 31*(4), 201–206.

Kid Sense Child Development Corporation. (2017). Gross motor skills. Retrieved from childdevelopment.com.au/areas-of-concern/gross-motor-skills /gross-motor-skills/

Kidd, C., Palmeri, H., & Aslin, R. N. (2013). Rational snacking: Young children's decision-making on the marshmallow task is moderated by beliefs about environmental reliability. *Cognition, 126*(1), 109–114. Retrieved from doi:10.1016 /j.cognition.2012.08.004

Kim, H., Byers, A. I., Cameron, C. E., Brock, L. L., Cottone, E. A., & Grissmer, D. W. (2016). Unique contributions of attentional control and visuomotor integration on concurrent teacher-reported classroom functioning in early elementary students. *Early Childhood Research Quarterly, 36*(3), 379–390. doi:10.1016 /j.ecresq.2016.01.018

Kim, H., & Cameron, C. E. (2016). Implications of visuospatial skills and executive functions for learning mathematics: Evidence from children with autism and Williams syndrome. *AERA Open, 2*(4). doi:10.1177/2332858416675124

Kim, H., Duran, C. A., Cameron, C. E., & Grissmer, D. W. (2017). Developmental relations among motor and cognitive processes and mathematics skills. *Child Development.* doi:10.1111/cdev.12752

Kim, H., Murrah, W. M., Cameron, C. E., Brock, L. L., Cottone, E. A., & Grissmer, D. (2015). Psychometric properties of the teacher-reported Motor Skills Rating Scale. *Journal of Psychoeducational Assessment, 33*(7), 640–651. doi:10.1177/0734282914551536

Kirk, M. A., & Rhodes, R. E. (2011). Motor skill interventions to improve fundamental movement skills of preschoolers with developmental delay. *Adapted Physical Activity Quarterly, 28*(3), 210–232.

Klein, A., Starkey, P., Clements, D., Sarama, J., & Iyer, R. (2008). Effects of a pre-kindergarten mathematics intervention: A randomized experiment. *Journal of Research on Educational Effectiveness, 1*(3), 155–178.

Kolkman, M. E., Kroesbergen, E. H., & Leseman, P. P. M. (2014). Involvement of working memory in longitudinal development of number–magnitude skills. *Infant and Child Development, 23*(1), 36–50. doi:10.1002/icd.1834

Kopp, C. B. (1982). Antecedents of self-regulation: A developmental perspective. *Developmental Psychology, 18*(2), 199–214.

Kopp, C. B. (1989). Regulation of distress and negative emotions: A developmental view. *Developmental Psychology, 25*(3), 343–354.

Korkman, M., Kemp, S., & Kirk, U. (2001). Developmental assessment of neuropsychological function with the aid of the NEPSY. In A. Kaufman & N. Kaufman (Eds.), *Specific learning disabilities and difficulties in children and adolescents: Psychological assessment and evaluation* (Cambridge Child and Adolescent Psychiatry, pp. 347–386). Cambridge, England: Cambridge University Press.

Krajewski, K., & Schneider, W. (2009). Exploring the impact of phonological awareness, visual-spatial working memory, and preschool quantity-number competencies on mathematics achievement in elementary school: Findings from a 3-year longitudinal study. *Journal of Experimental Child Psychology, 103*(4), 516–531. doi:10.1016/j.jecp.2009.03.009

Kroesbergen, E. H., Van Luit, J. E. H., Van Lieshout, E. C. D. M., Van Loosbroek, E., & Van de Rijt, B. A. M. (2009). Individual differences in early numeracy: The role of executive functions and subitizing. *Journal of Psychoeducational Assessment, 27*(3), 226–236.

Ladd, G. W., Birch, S. H., & Buhs, E. S. (1999). Children's social and scholastic lives in kindergarten: Related spheres of influence? *Child Development, 70*(6), 1373–1400.

Laski, E. V., & Siegler, R. S. (2014). Learning from number board games: You learn what you encode. *Developmental Psychology, 50*(3), 853–864. doi:10.1037/a0034321

Latash, M., Wood, L., & Ulrich, D. (2008). *What is currently known about hypotonia, motor skill development, and physical activity in Down syndrome.* Paper prepared from presentations and discussions at the Down Syndrome Research Directions Symposium 2007, Portsmouth, England. Retrieved from www.dseinternational.org/research-directions/

LeFevre, J.-A., Fast, L., Skwarchuk, S.-L., Smith-Chant, B. L., Bisanz, J., Kamawar, D., & Penner-Wilger, M. (2010). Pathways to mathematics: Longitudinal predictors of performance. *Child Development, 81*(6), 1753–1767. doi:10.1111/j.1467-8624.2010.01508.x

Levine, S. C., Huttenlocher, J., Taylor, A., & Langrock, A. (1999). Early sex differences in spatial skill. *Developmental Psychology, 35*(4), 940–949.

Liew, J., Chen, Q., & Hughes, J. N. (2010). Child effortful control, teacher-student relationships, and achievement in academically at-risk children: Additive and interactive effects. *Early Childhood Research Quarterly, 25*(1), 51–64. doi:10.1016/j.ecresq.2009.07.005

Lillard, A. S. (2005). *Montessori: The science behind the genius.* New York, NY: Oxford University Press.

LoCasale-Crouch, J., Konold, T., Pianta, R., Howes, C., Burchinal, M., Bryant, D., . . . Barbarin, O. (2007). Observed classroom quality profiles in state-funded pre-kindergarten programs and associations with teacher, program, and classroom characteristics. *Early Childhood Research Quarterly, 22*(1), 3–17. doi:10.1016/j.ecresq.2006.05.001

Loo, S. K., & Rapport, M. D. (1998). Ethnic variations in children's problem behaviors: A cross-sectional, developmental study of Hawaii school children. *Journal of Child Psychology and Psychiatry, 39*(4), 567–575.

Lu, C., & Montague, B. (2016). Move to learn, learn to move: Prioritizing physical activity in early childhood education programming. *Early Childhood Education Journal, 44*(5), 409–417. doi:10.1007/s10643-015-0730-5

Manfra, L., Davis, K. D., Ducenne, L., & Winsler, A. (2014). Preschoolers' motor and verbal self-control strategies during a resistance-to-temptation task. *The Journal of Genetic Psychology, 175*(4), 332–345. doi:10.1080/00221325.201 4.917067

Marr, D., Cermak, S., Cohn, E. S., & Henderson, A. (2003). Fine motor activities in Head Start and kindergarten classrooms. *American Journal of Occupational Therapy, 57*(5), 550–557. doi:10.5014/ajot.57.5.550

Martin, R., Tigera, C., Denckla, M. B., & Mahone, E. M. (2010). Factor structure of paediatric timed motor examination and its relationship with IQ. *Developmental Medicine & Child Neurology, 52*(8), e188–e194.

Mashburn, A. J., Hamre, B. K., Downer, J. T., & Pianta, R. C. (2006). Teacher and classroom characteristics associated with teachers' ratings of prekindergartners' relationships and behaviors. *Journal of Psychoeducational Assessment, 24*(4), 367–380. doi:10.1177/0734282906290594

Mashburn, A. J., Pianta, R. C., Hamre, B. K., Downer, J. T., Barbarin, O. A., Bryant, D., . . . Howes, C. (2008). Measures of classroom quality in prekindergarten and children's development of academic, language, and social skills. *Child Development, 79*(3), 732–749. doi:10.1111/j.1467-8624.2008.01154.x

Mason, B. A., Gunersel, A. B., & Ney, E. A. (2014). Cultural and ethnic bias in teacher ratings of behavior: A criterion-focused review. *Psychology in the Schools, 51*(10), 1017–1030. doi:10.1002/pits.21800

McCabe, L. A., Rebello-Britto, P., Hernandez, M., & Brooks-Gunn, J. (2004). Games children play: Observing young children's self-regulation across laboratory, home, and school settings. In R. DelCarmen-Wiggins & A. Carter (Eds.), *Handbook of infant, toddler, and preschool mental health assessment* (pp. 491–521). New York, NY: Oxford University Press.

McCarron, L. T. (1997). *McCarron assessment of neuromuscular development* (3rd ed.). Dallas, TX: McCarron-Dial Systems.

McClelland, M. M., & Cameron, C. E. (2012). Self-regulation in early childhood: Improving conceptual clarity and developing ecologically valid measures. *Child Development Perspectives, 6*(2), 136–142. doi:10.1111/j.1750-8606 .2011.00191.x

McClelland, M. M., Cameron, C. E., Connor, C. M., Farris, C. L., Jewkes, A. M., & Morrison, F. J. (2007). Links between behavioral regulation and preschoolers' literacy, vocabulary, and math skills. *Developmental Psychology, 43*(4), 947–959. doi:10.1037/0012-1649.43.4.947

McClelland, M. M., Cameron, C. E., Duncan, R., Bowles, R. P., Acock, A. C., Miao, A., & Pratt, M. E. (2014). Predictors of early growth in academic achievement: The Head-Toes-Knees-Shoulders task. *Frontiers in Psychology, 5*. doi:10.3389 /fpsyg.2014.00599

McClelland, M. M., Cameron, C. E., Wanless, S. B., & Murray, A. (2007). Executive function, behavioral self-regulation, and social-emotional competence: Links to school readiness. In O. N. Saracho & B. Spodek (Eds.), *Contemporary perspectives in early childhood education: Social learning in early childhood education* (Vol. 7, pp. 113–137). Greenwich, CT: Information Age Publishing.

McClelland, M. M., Cameron Ponitz, C. E., Messersmith, E. E., & Tominey, S. L. (2010). Self-regulation: The integration of cognition and emotion. In R. M. Lerner & W. F. Overton (Eds.), *The handbook of life-span development, Vol. 1: Cognition, biology, and methods* (pp. 509–553). New York, NY: Wiley & Sons.

McConnell, D., Breitkreuz, R., & Savage, A. (2011). From financial hardship to child difficulties: Main and moderating effects of perceived social support. *Child: Care, Health and Development, 37*(5), 679–691. doi:10.1111/j.1365 -2214.2010.01185.x

McDermott, P. A., Leigh, N. M., & Perry, M. A. (2002). Development and validation of the preschool learning behaviors scale. *Psychology in the Schools, 39*(4), 353–365. doi:10.1002/pits.10036

McIntyre, F., Parker, H., Thornton, A., Licari, M., Piek, J., Rigoli, D., & Hands, B. (2017). Assessing motor proficiency in young adults: The Bruininks Os-eretsky Test-2 Short Form and the McCarron Assessment of Neuromuscular Development. *Human Movement Science, 53*, 55–62. doi:10.1016/j.humov .2016.10.004

McWayne, C. M., Cheung, K., Wright, L. E. G., & Hahs-Vaughn, D. L. (2012). Patterns of school readiness among head start children: Meaningful within-group variability during the transition to kindergarten. *Journal of Educational Psychology, 104*(3), 862–878. doi:10.1037/a0028884

Medwell, J., Strand, S., & Wray, D. (2007). The role of handwriting in composing for Y2 children. *Journal of Reading, Writing and Literacy, 2*(1), 11–21.

Medwell, J., Strand, S., & Wray, D. (2009). The links between handwriting and composing for Y6 children. *Cambridge Journal of Education, 39*(3), 329–344.

Medwell, J., & Wray, D. (2014). Handwriting automaticity: The search for performance thresholds. *Language and Education, 28*(1), 34–51. doi:10.1080 /09500782.2013.763819

Meisels, S. J., Marsden, D. B., Wiske, M. S., & Henderson, L. W. (2008). *The early screening inventory—Revised*. San Antonio, TX: Pearson.

Merritt, E. G., Wanless, S. B., Rimm-Kaufman, S. E., Cameron, C. E., & Peugh, J. L. (2012). The contributions of teachers' emotional support to children's social behaviors and self-regulatory skills in first grade. *School Psychology Review, 41*(2), 141–159.

Miller, H. E., Vlach, H. A., & Simmering, V. R. (2016). Producing spatial words is not enough: Understanding the relation between language and spatial cognition. *Child Development, 88,* 1966–1982. doi:10.1111/cdev.12664

Mix, K. S., & Cheng, Y.-L. (2012). The relation between space and math: Developmental and educational implications. *Advances in Child Development and Behavior, 42,* 197–243.

Miyake, A., Friedman, N. P., Emerson, M. J., Witzki, A. H., & Howerter, A. (2000). The unity and diversity of executive functions and their contributions to complex "frontal lobe" tasks: A latent variable analysis. *Cognitive Psychology, 41*(1), 49-100. doi:10.1006/cogp.1999.0734

Miyake, A., Friedman, N. P., Rettinger, D. A., Shah, P., & Hegarty, M. (2001). How are visuospatial working memory, executive functioning, and spatial abilities related? A latent-variable analysis. *Journal of Experimental Psychology: General, 130*(4), 621–640.

Monti, J. M., Hillman, C. H., & Cohen, N. J. (2012). Aerobic fitness enhances relational memory in preadolescent children: The FITKids randomized control trial. *Hippocampus, 22*(9), 1876–1882. doi:10.1002/hipo.22023

Morris, P., Millenky, M., Raver, C. C., & Jones, S. M. (2014). Does a preschool social and emotional learning intervention pay off for classroom instruction and children's behavior and academic skills? Evidence from the Foundations of Learning project. *Early Education and Development, 24*(7), 1020–1042. doi: 10.1080/10409289.2013.825187

Morrison, F. J., Bachman, H. J., & Connor, C. M. (2005). *Improving literacy in America: Guidelines from research.* New Haven, CT: Yale University Press.

Morrison, F. J., & Grammer, J. K. (2016). Conceptual clutter and measurement mayhem: A proposal for a cross disciplinary approach to conceptualizing and measuring executive function. In J. A. Griffin, L. S. Freund, & P. McArdle (Eds.), *Executive function in preschool age children: Integrating measurement, neurodevelopment and translational research* (pp. 327–348). Washington, DC: American Psychological Association.

Murrah, W. M. (2010). *Comparing self-regulatory and early academic skills as predictors of later math, reading, and science elementary school achievement* (Doctoral dissertation). Available from ProQuest Information & Learning.

National Education Goals Panel. (1995). *Reconsidering children's early development and learning: Toward common views and vocabulary.* Retrieved from govinfo.library.unt.edu/negp/reports/child-ea.htm

National Reading Panel (NRP). (2000). *Teaching children to read: An evidence-based assessment of the scientific research literature on reading and its implications for reading instruction (Summary).* Bethesda, MD, USA: National Institute of Child Health and Human Development (NIH). Retrieved from www.nichd.nih.gov/publications/pubs/nrp/Documents/report.pdf

Netelenbos, J. B. (2005). Teachers' ratings of gross motor skills suffer from low concurrent validity. *Human Movement Science, 24*(1), 116–137. doi:10.1016/j.humov.2005.02.001

Nickerson, A. B., & Fishman, C. (2009). Convergent and divergent validity of the Devereux Student Strengths Assessment. *School Psychology Quarterly, 24*(1), 48–59. doi:10.1037/a0015147

Noah, T. (2010). The United States of inequality. Retrieved from www.slate.com /articles/news_and_politics/the_great_divergence/features/2010/the_united _states_of_inequality/introducing_the_great_divergence.html

Ogawa, K., Erato, C. N., & Inui, T. (2010). Brain mechanisms of visuomotor transformation based on deficits in tracing and copying. *Japanese Psychological Research, 52*(2), 91–106. doi:10.1111/j.1468-5884.2010.00427.x

Pagani, L. S., & Messier, S. (2012). Links between motor skills and indicators of school readiness at kindergarten entry in urban disadvantaged children. *Journal of Educational and Developmental Psychology, 2*(1), 95–107. doi:10.5539/ jedp.v2n1p95

Parameswaran, G. (2003). Age, gender and training in children's performance of Piaget's horizontality task. *Educational Studies, 29*(2–3), 307–319. doi:10.1080/03055690303272

Penner, A. M. (2014). Can we expect more of teachers? Comment on Robinson-Cimpian, Lubienski, Ganley, and Copur-Gencturk (2014). *Developmental Psychology, 50*(4), 1285–1287. doi:10.1037/a0035326

Piaget, J. (1963). *The origins of intelligence in children.* New York, NY: W. W. Norton.

Pianta, R. C., Cox, M. J., & Snow, K. L. (2007). *School readiness and the transition to kindergarten in the era of accountability.* Baltimore, MD: Brookes.

Pianta, R. C., Howes, C., Burchinal, M., Bryant, D., Clifford, R., Early, D., & Barbarin, O. (2005). Features of pre-kindergarten programs, classrooms, and teachers: Do they predict observed classroom quality and child-teacher interactions? *Applied Developmental Science, 9*(3), 144–159. doi:10.1207 /s1532480xads0903_2

Piek, J. P., Dyck, M. J., Nieman, A., Anderson, M., Hay, D., Smith, L. M., . . . Hallmayer, J. (2004). The relationship between motor coordination, executive functioning and attention in school aged children. *Archives of Clinical Neuropsychology, 19*(8), 1063–1076. doi:10.1016/j.acn.2003.12.007

Pless, M., & Carlsson, M. (2000). Effects of motor skill intervention on developmental coordination disorder: A meta-analysis. *Adapted Physical Activity Quarterly, 17*(4), 381–401.

Potter, D., Mashburn, A., & Grissmer, D. W. (2012). The family, neuroscience, and academic skills: An interdisciplinary account of social class gaps in children's test scores. *Social Science Research, 42*(2), 446–464. doi:10.1016/j .ssresearch.2012.09.009

Pruden, S. M., Levine, S. C., & Huttenlocher, J. (2011). Children's spatial thinking: Does talk about the spatial world matter? *Developmental Science, 14*(6), 1417–1430. doi:10.1111/j.1467-7687.2011.01088.x

Purpura, D. J., Schmitt, S. A., & Ganley, C. M. (2017). Foundations of mathematics and literacy: The role of executive functioning components. *Journal of Experimental Child Psychology, 153*, 15–34. doi:10.1016/j.jecp.2016.08.010

Ramani, G. B., & Siegler, R. S. (2008). Promoting broad and stable improvements in low-income children's numerical knowledge through playing number board games. *Child Development, 79*(2), 375–394.

Ramani, G. B., & Siegler, R. S. (2011). Reducing the gap in numerical knowledge between low- and middle-income preschoolers. *Journal of Applied Developmental Psychology, 32*(3), 146–159. doi:10.1016/j.appdev.2011.02.005

Ramani, G. B., Siegler, R. S., & Hitti, A. (2012). Taking it to the classroom: Number board games as a small group learning activity. *Journal of Educational Psychology, 104*(3), 661–672. doi:10.1037/a0028995

Rapport, M. D., Orban, S. A., Kofler, M. J., & Friedman, L. M. (2013). Do programs designed to train working memory, other executive functions, and attention benefit children with ADHD? A meta-analytic review of cognitive, academic, and behavioral outcomes. *Clinical Psychology Review, 33*(8), 1237–1252. doi:10.1016/j.cpr.2013.08.005

Raver, C. C., Jones, S. M., Li-Grining, C. P., Zhai, F., Bub, K., & Pressler, E. (2011). CSRP's impact on low-income preschoolers' preacademic skills: Self-regulation as a mediating mechanism. *Child Development, 82*(1), 362–378. doi:10.1111/j.1467-8624.2010.01561.x

Ready, D. D., & Chu, E. M. (2015). Sociodemographic inequality in early literacy development: The role of teacher perceptual accuracy. *Early Education and Development, 26*(7), 970–987. doi:10.1080/10409289.2015.1004516

Ready, D. D., LoGerfo, L. F., Burkam, D. T., & Lee, V. E. (2005). Explaining girls' advantage in kindergarten literacy learning: Do classroom behaviors make a difference? *Elementary School Journal, 106*(1), 21–38. doi:10.1086/496905

Rebello Britto, P., & Limlingan, M. C. (2012). *School readiness and transitions.* New York, NY, USA: UNICEF, Division of Communication. Retrieved from www.unicef.org/publications/files/CFS_School_Readiness_E_web.pdf

Reid, J. L., & Kagan, S. L. (2014). *A better start: Why classroom diversity matters in early education.* Retrieved from www.tcf.org/bookstore/detail/a-better-start

Resnick, S. M., Gottesman, I. I., & McGue, M. (1993). Sensation seeking in opposite-sex twins: An effect of prenatal hormones? *Behavior Genetics, 23*(4), 323–329.

Riethmuller, A. M., Jones, R. A., & Okely, A. D. (2009). Efficacy of interventions to improve motor development in young children: A systematic review. *Pediatrics, 124*(4), e782–e792. doi:10.1542/peds.2009-0333

Rimm-Kaufman, S., Pianta, R. C., & Cox, M. J. (2000). Teachers' judgments of problems in the transition to kindergarten. *Early Childhood Research Quarterly, 15*(2), 147–166.

Roeber, B. J., Tober, C. L., Bolt, D. M., & Pollak, S. D. (2012). Gross motor development in children adopted from orphanage settings. *Developmental Medicine and Child Neurology, 54*(6), 527–531. doi:10.1111/j.1469-8749.2012.04257.x

Roman, A. S., Pisoni, D. B., & Kronenberger, W. G. (2014). Assessment of working memory capacity in preschool children using the Missing Scan Task. *Infant and Child Development, 23*(6), 575–587. doi:10.1002/icd.1849

Roskos, K. A., & Burstein, K. (2013). Print to pixel: Foundations of an e-book instructional model in early literacy. In A. Shamir & O. Korat (Eds.), *Technology as a support for literacy achievements for children at risk* (pp. 47–58). Dordrecht, Netherlands: Springer.

Roth, A., Kim, H., & Care, E. (2017). New data on the breadth of skills movement: Over 150 countries included. Retrieved from www.brookings.edu/blog/education-plus-development/2017/08/31/new-data-on-the-breadth-of-skills-movement-over-150-countries-included/

Rothbart, M. K., Posner, M. I., & Kieras, J. (2006). Temperament, attention, and the development of self-regulation. In K. McCartney & D. Phillips (Eds.), *Blackwell handbook of early childhood development* (pp. 338–357). Malden, MA: Blackwell Publishing.

Rutter, M. (2013). Annual research review: Resilience—clinical implications. *Journal of Child Psychology and Psychiatry, 54*(4), 474–487. doi:10.1111/j.1469 -7610.2012.02615.x

Sarama, J., Clements, D. H., Starkey, P., Klein, A., & Wakeley, A. (2008). Scaling up the implementation of a pre-kindergarten mathematics curriculum: Teaching for understanding with trajectories and technologies. *Journal of Research on Educational Effectiveness, 1*(2), 89–119.

Sarama, J., Lange, A. A., Clements, D. H., & Wolfe, C. B. (2012). The impacts of an early mathematics curriculum on oral language and literacy. *Early Childhood Research Quarterly, 27*(3), 489–502. doi:10.1016/j.ecresq.2011.12.002

Sattelmair, J., & Ratey, J. J. (2009). *Physically active play and cognition: An academic matter*. Champaign-Urbana, IL: The Board of Trustees of the University of Illinois. Retrieved from www.journalofplay.org/issues/1/3/article /physically-active-play-and-cognition-academic-matter

Schoemaker, M. M., Niemeijer, A. S., Flapper, B. C. T., & Smits-Engelsman, B. C. M. (2012). Validity and reliability of the Movement Assessment Battery for Children-2 checklist for children with and without motor impairments. *Developmental Medicine & Child Neurology, 54*(4), 368–375. doi:10.1111/j.1469-8749.2012.04226.x

Scott, J. P. (1962). Critical periods in behavioral development. *Science, 138*(3544), 949–958.

Scott-Little, C., Kagan, S. L., & Frelow, V. S. (2006). Conceptualization of readiness and the content of early learning standards: The intersection of policy and research? *Early Childhood Research Quarterly, 21*(2), 153–173. doi:10.1016/j. ecresq.2006.04.003

Screws, D. P., Eason, B. L., & Surburg, P. R. (1998). Crossing the midline: A study of four-year-old children. *Perceptual Motor Skills, 86*(1), 201–203. doi:10.2466 /pms.1998.86.1.201

Seashore, R. H., Buxton, C. E., & McCollom, I. N. (1940). Multiple factorial analysis of fine motor skills. *The American Journal of Psychology, 53*(2), 251–259. doi:10.2307/1417420

Shah, P., & Miyake, A. (1996). The separability of working memory resources for spatial thinking and language processing: An individual differences approach. *Journal of Experimental Psychology: General, 125*(1), 4–27.

Shalaby, C. (2017). *Troublemakers: Lessons in freedom from young children at school*. New York, NY: The New Press.

Shonkoff, J. P., & Phillips, D. A. (2000). *From neurons to neighborhoods: The science of early childhood development*. Washington, DC: National Academy Press.

Siegler, R. S., & Ramani, G. B. (2009). Playing linear number board games—but not circular ones—improves low-income preschoolers numerical understanding. *Journal of Educational Psychology, 101*(3), 545–560. doi:10.1037/a0014239

Sigmundsson, H., Whiting, H. T., & Loftesnes, J. M. (2000). Development of proprioceptive sensitivity. *Experimental Brain Research, 135*(3), 348–352.

Skinner, R. A., & Piek, J. P. (2001). Psychosocial implications of poor motor coordination in children and adolescents. *Human Movement Science, 20*(1–2), 73–94. doi:10.1016/S0167-9457(01)00029-X

Smith, E. E., Jonides, J., & Koeppe, R. A. (1996). Dissociating verbal and spatial working memory using PET. *Cereb Cortex, 6*(1), 11–20.

Son, S.-H., & Meisels, S. J. (2006). The relationship of young children's motor skills to later reading and math achievement. *Merrill-Palmer Quarterly, 52*(4), 755–778. doi:10.1353/mpq.2006.0033

Soska, K. C., Adolph, K. E., & Johnson, S. P. (2010). Systems in development: Motor skill acquisition facilitates three-dimensional object completion. *Developmental Psychology, 46*(1), 129–138.

Stins, J. F., Sonneville, L. M. J., Groot, A. S., Polderman, T. C., Baal, C. G. C. M., & Boomsma, D. I. (2005). Heritability of selective attention and working memory in preschoolers. *Behavior Genetics, 35*(4), 407–416. doi:10.1007/s10519-004-3875-3

Stipek, D. J., Feiler, R., Daniels, D., & Milburn, S. (1995). Effects of different instructional approaches on young children's achievement and motivation. *Child Development, 66*(1), 209–223. doi:10.2307/1131201

Stumpf, H., Mills, C. J., Brody, L. E., & Baxley, P. G. (2013). Expanding talent search procedures by including measures of spatial ability: CTY's Spatial Test Battery. *Roeper Review, 35*(4), 254–264. doi:10.1080/02783193.2013.829548

Suggate, S. P., & Stoeger, H. (2014). Do nimble hands make for nimble lexicons? Fine motor skills predict knowledge of embodied vocabulary items. *First Language, 34*(3), 244–261. doi:10.1177/0142723714535768

Thelen, E. (2005). Dynamic systems theory and the complexity of change. *Psychoanalytic Dialogues, 15*(2), 255–283. doi:10.1080/10481881509348831

Thompson, J. M., Nuerk, H.-C., Moeller, K., & Cohen Kadosh, R. (2013). The link between mental rotation ability and basic numerical representations. *Acta Psychologica, 144*(2), 324–331. doi:10.1016/j.actpsy.2013.05.009

Tominey, S. L., & McClelland, M. M. (2011). Red light, purple light: Findings from a randomized trial using circle time games to improve behavioral self-regulation in preschool. *Early Education & Development, 22*(3), 489–519. doi:10.1080/10409289.2011.574258

Tseng, V. (2012). The uses of research in policy and practice. *Social Policy Report: Sharing Child and Youth Development Knowledge, 26*(2). Retrieved from files.eric.ed.gov/fulltext/ED536954.pdf

Uttal, D. H., Meadow, N. G., Tipton, E., Hand, L. L., Alden, A. R., Warren, C., & Newcombe, N. S. (2013). The malleability of spatial skills: A meta-analysis of training studies. *Psychological Bulletin, 139*(2), 352–402. doi:10.1037/a0028446

Veldman, S. L. C., Jones, R. A., & Okely, A. D. (2016). Efficacy of gross motor skill interventions in young children: An updated systematic review. *BMJ Open Sport & Exercise Medicine, 2*(1). doi:10.1136/bmjsem-2015-000067

Verdine, B. N., Golinkoff, R. M., Hirsh-Pasek, K., & Newcombe, N. S. (2017). II. Methods for longitudinal study of preschool spatial and mathematical skills. *Monographs of the Society for Research in Child Development, 82*(1), 31–55. doi:10.1111/mono.12281

Verdine, B. N., Irwin, C. M., Golinkoff, R. M., & Hirsh-Pasek, K. (2014). Contributions of executive function and spatial skills to preschool mathematics achievement. *Journal of Experimental Child Psychology, 126*, 37–51. doi:10.1016/j .jecp.2014.02.012

Visser, J. (2003). Developmental coordination disorder: A review of research on subtypes and comorbidities. *Human Movement Science, 22*(4–5), 479–493. doi:10.1016/j.humov.2003.09.005

Vitiello, V. E., Greenfield, D. B., Munis, P., & George, J. L. (2011). Cognitive flexibility, approaches to learning, and academic school readiness in Head Start preschool children. *Early Education and Development, 22*(3), 388–410. doi: 10.1080/10409289.2011.538366

Vygotsky, L. S. (1978). *Mind in society: The development of higher psychological processes*. Cambridge, MA: Harvard University Press.

Wai, J., Lubinski, D., & Benbow, C. P. (2009). Spatial ability for STEM domains: Aligning over 50 years of cumulative psychological knowledge solidifies its importance. *Journal of Educational Psychology, 101*(4), 817–835. doi:10.1037 /a0016127

Wasik, B. A., Hindman, A. H., & Snell, E. K. (2016). Book reading and vocabulary development: A systematic review. *Early Childhood Research Quarterly, 37*(Supplement C), 39–57. doi:10.1016/j.ecresq.2016.04.003

Weisberg, D. S., Hirsh-Pasek, K., & Golinkoff, R. M. (2013). Guided play: Where curricular goals meet a playful pedagogy. *Mind, Brain, and Education, 7*(2), 104–112. doi:10.1111/mbe.12015

Weisner, T. S. (1996). The 5 to 7 transition as an ecocultural project. In A. J. Sameroff & M. M. Haith (Eds.), *The five to seven year shift: The age of reason and responsibility* (pp. 295–326). Chicago, IL: University of Chicago Press.

Wesley, P. W., & Buysse, V. (2003). Making meaning of school readiness in schools and communities. *Early Childhood Research Quarterly, 18*(3), 351–375. doi:10.1016/S0885-2006(03)00044-9

White, R. E. (2013). *The power of play: A research summary on play and learning*. Minneapolis, MN, USA: Minnesota Children's Museum. Retrieved from www. childrensmuseums.org/images/MCMResearchSummary.pdf

Whitehurst, G. J. R. (2016). Hard thinking on soft skills. Washington, DC: Brookings Institute. Retrieved from www.brookings.edu/wp-content/uploads/2016/07 /Download-the-paper2.pdf

Wiart, L., & Darrah, J. (2001). Review of four tests of gross motor development. *Developmental Medicine & Child Neurology, 43*(4), 279–285. doi:10.1111 /j.1469-8749.2001.tb00204.x

Wiebe, S. A., Sheffield, T., Nelson, J. M., Clark, C. A. C., Chevalier, N., & Espy, K. A. (2011). The structure of executive function in 3-year-olds. *Journal of Experimental Child Psychology, 108*(3), 436–452.

Williford, A. P., Downer, J. T., & Hamre, B. K. (2013). *The Virginia Kindergarten Readiness Project: Concurrent validity of Teaching Strategies GOLD Phase 1 Report*. Charlottesville, VA: University of Virginia. Retrieved from www.e3va .org/wp-content/uploads/2014/02/VKRP-Validity-Report_2014.pdf

Williford, A. P., LoCasale-Crouch, J., Whittaker, J. V., DeCoster, J., Hartz, K. A., Carter, L. M., . . . Hatfield, B. E. (2016). Changing teacher–child dyadic interactions to improve preschool children's externalizing behaviors. *Child Development, 88*(5), 1544–1553. doi:10.1111/cdev.12703

Willingham, D. B. (1998). A neuropsychological theory of motor skill learning. *Psychological Review, 105*(3), 558–584. doi:10.1037/0033-295X.105.3.558

Willoughby, M. T., Blair, C., Wirth, R. J., & Greenberg, M. (2012). The measurement of executive function at age 5: Psychometric properties and relationship to academic achievement. *Psychological Assessment, 24*(1), 226–239. doi:10.1037/a0025361

Willoughby, M. T., Wirth, R. J., & Blair, C. (2011). Contributions of modern measurement theory to measuring executive function in early childhood: An empirical demonstration. *Journal of Experimental Child Psychology, 108*(3), 414–435.

Wilson, A., Piek, J. P., & Kane, R. (2013). The mediating role of social skills in the relationship between motor ability and internalizing symptoms in preprimary children. *Infant and Child Development, 22*(2), 151–164. doi:10.1002/icd.1773

Winsler, A., Diaz, R. M., Atencio, D. J., McCarthy, E. M., & Adams Chabay, L. (2000). Verbal self-regulation over time in preschool children at risk for attention and behavior problems. *Journal of Child Psychology and Psychiatry, 41*(7), 875–886.

Winthrop, R., Williams, T. P., & McGivney, E. (2016). Accelerating progress in education with hands-on, minds-on learning. Retrieved from www.brookings.edu/blog/education-plus-development/2016/07/14/accelerating-progress-in-education-with-hands-on-minds-on-learning/

Wolff, P. H., Gunnoe, C., & Cohen, C. (1985). Neuromotor maturation and psychological performance: A developmental study. *Developmental Medicine and Child Neurology, 27*(3), 344–354.

Wood, D., Bruner, J. S., & Ross, G. (1976). The role of tutoring in problem solving. *Journal of Child Psychology and Psychiatry, 17*(2), 89–100.

Wright, T. S. (2011). Countering the politics of class, race, gender, and geography in early childhood education. *Educational Policy, 25*(1), 240–261. doi:10.1177/0895904810387414

Wuang, Y., Wang, C., Huang, M., & Su, C. (2008). Profiles and cognitive predictors of motor functions among early school-age children with mild intellectual disabilities. *Journal of Intellectual Disability Research, 52*(Part 12), 1048–1060.

Zacks, J. M., Mires, J., Tversky, B., & Hazeltine, E. (2001). Mental spatial transformations of objects and perspective. *Spatial Cognition and Computation, 2*(4), 315–332. doi:10.1023/a:1015584100204

Zelazo, P. D. (2015). Executive function: Reflection, iterative reprocessing, complexity, and the developing brain. *Developmental Review, 38*, 55–68. doi:10.1016/j.dr.2015.07.001

Zelazo, P. D., Carlson, S. M., & Kesek, A. (2008). The development of executive function in childhood. In C. A. Nelson & M. Luciana (Eds.), *Handbook of developmental cognitive neuroscience* (2nd ed., pp. 553–574). Cambridge, MA: MIT Press.

Zelazo, P. D., Carter, A., Reznick, J. S., & Frye, D. (1997). Early development of executive function: A problem-solving framework. *Review of General Psychology, 1*(2), 198–226.

Index

A letter *f* or *t* after a page number refers to a figure or table, respectively.

About the Author

Claire E. Cameron is associate professor in the Department of Learning and Instruction at the University at Buffalo. She directs the Early Childhood and Childhood programs for teachers seeking certification to teach in New York State, and for researchers seeking a doctorate with a preschool or elementary focus. She is an expert in the development and assessment of foundational cognitive skills in early childhood and author of the Head-Toes-Knees-Shoulders (HTKS) behavioral assessment and the Motor Skills Rating Scale (MSRS) teacher-report questionnaire. Cameron earned her PhD in 2007 from the University of Michigan's Combined Program in Education and Psychology in Ann Arbor. She was an Institute for Education Sciences Postdoctoral Fellow from 2007 to 2009 at the University of Virginia's Center for Advanced Study of Teaching & Learning (CASTL), where she stayed on as research scientist until moving to Buffalo in 2015. She is a passionate proponent of translating research for public audiences and serves on the advisory board for the University of Connecticut's PK–3 Leadership Program. Learn more about Cameron's work at claireelizabethcameron.com.